Internal Family Systems Made Simple

A Beginner's Path to Understanding Your Multiple Parts, Healing Emotional Pain, and Transforming Your Inner World

I0145018

Kieran Tina Miles

ISBN: 978-1-7643835-8-5

First Edition, 2025

This book is designed to provide information about Internal Family Systems therapy and related psychological concepts for educational purposes. It is sold with the understanding that the publisher and author are not engaged in rendering psychological, medical, or other professional services. If expert assistance or counseling is needed, the services of a competent professional should be sought.

The examples and case studies presented in this book are fictional composites created for illustrative purposes. Any resemblance to actual persons, living or dead, or actual events is purely coincidental. Names, characters, situations, and details have been changed or invented to protect privacy and illustrate therapeutic concepts. No individual case represents a real person or actual therapeutic relationship.

The information presented is based on the Internal Family Systems model developed by Dr. Richard C. Schwartz and represents the author's understanding and interpretation of publicly available information about this therapeutic approach. This book is not affiliated with, endorsed by, or sponsored by the IFS Institute or Dr. Richard C. Schwartz. Readers interested in official IFS training or certification should contact the IFS Institute directly.

While Internal Family Systems has shown promise in research studies and clinical practice, individual results may vary. This book is not intended to diagnose, treat, cure, or prevent any mental health condition. The techniques described should not replace professional

Table of Contents

About The Author

As a registered mental health professional, I've spent years watching people struggle with the same painful patterns—anxiety that won't quit, relationships that repeat the same conflicts, behaviors they desperately want to change but can't seem to stop. When I discovered Internal Family Systems therapy, I saw something remarkable: people weren't just managing their symptoms anymore. They were actually healing.

But there was a problem.

Most IFS resources were written for therapists, packed with clinical terminology and theoretical frameworks that made perfect sense to professionals but left everyday people lost and confused. I watched clients light up when I explained IFS concepts in simple language, then struggle to find books they could actually understand when they wanted to learn more.

That's why I wrote this book.

I believe everyone deserves access to powerful healing tools, not just people who can decode psychology textbooks. I believe that understanding your internal world shouldn't require a graduate degree in counseling. And I believe the most profound psychological insights can be explained in language that sounds like a conversation with a trusted friend rather than a lecture from an academic.

Throughout these pages, you'll find: clear explanations, relatable examples, and practical tools you can start using immediately. No confusing jargon. No dense theory. Just honest guidance for understanding why you are the way you are—and how to become who you want to be.

Your internal family has been waiting for someone to explain things in a way that actually makes sense. This book is that explanation.

Kieran Tina Miles
Registered Mental Health Professional

Preface

You've probably been told at some point that you need to "get rid of" the parts of yourself you don't like. Eliminate your anxiety. Stop being so critical. Control your impulses. Fix what's broken.

This book takes a radically different approach.

What if nothing about you needs to be eliminated? What if the anxiety, the criticism, the behaviors you wish you could change— what if they're all trying to help you in the only ways they know how?

This idea changed everything for me when I first encountered Internal Family Systems therapy. Instead of fighting myself, I started getting curious about myself. Instead of trying to shut down the critical voice in my head, I asked it what it was afraid of. Instead of hating the parts of me that seemed self-destructive, I wondered what pain they were trying to protect me from.

The answers I found were surprising, heartbreaking, and ultimately liberating.

I wrote this book for everyone who's tired of being at war with themselves. For people who've tried to think their way out of anxiety, logic their way out of depression, or willpower their way out of patterns that keep repeating. For anyone who's ever wondered why they can't seem to change, even when they desperately want to.

The Internal Family Systems model offers something rare in the world of psychology and self-help: a framework that treats every part of you with respect and curiosity, even the parts that cause problems. It recognizes that you're not broken—you're a complex system doing its best to survive and thrive with the strategies it learned along the way.

1

This book is written for complete beginners. You don't need any background in psychology or therapy. You don't need to have your life in crisis to benefit from this approach. You just need to be willing to get curious about your inner world.

Throughout these pages, you'll meet people dealing with everyday struggles—anxiety about work presentations, relationship conflicts, depression, self-criticism, behaviors they can't seem to stop. You'll see how understanding their internal families helped them make sense of patterns that had confused them for years.

More importantly, you'll learn practical tools for working with your own parts. The 6 F's protocol, the unburdening process, and daily practices that help you access the calm, compassionate Self that's been inside you all along.

This journey isn't about becoming a different person. It's about becoming more fully yourself—the you that exists underneath all the protection, all the old wounds, all the strategies that made sense once but don't serve you anymore.

Your internal family has been waiting for this conversation. They're ready to be heard, understood, and guided by the wise leader you already are.

Let's begin.

Chapter 1: IFS Basics

Have you ever had a conversation with yourself? You know the kind—where one voice in your head says "Go for it!" while another screams "Are you crazy? Stay safe!" Or maybe you've noticed that sometimes you feel like a completely different person depending on the situation. At work, you're confident and organized. At your parents' house, you turn into an awkward teenager again. With your best friend, you're carefree and funny.

If this sounds familiar, congratulations—you're completely normal. In fact, you're experiencing what Internal Family Systems therapy calls "parts."

What Is Internal Family Systems Therapy?

Internal Family Systems, or IFS for short, is a type of therapy developed by a psychologist named Richard Schwartz back in the 1980s. The basic idea is simple but powerful: your mind isn't just one single thing. Instead, you have different parts of yourself, kind of like members of a family living inside you. These parts have different personalities, different ages, different jobs, and sometimes they don't get along with each other.

Think of it like this: Imagine your mind is a house, and different parts of you live in different rooms. Sometimes they're all cooperating, working together to help you navigate your day. Other times, they're fighting for control, each one convinced they know what's best for you.

The best part? IFS says this is totally normal. You're not broken. You're not weird. You're not crazy. You're just human.

You're Not Broken, You're Just Multiple

For years, psychology treated people as if they should have one unified personality, one consistent way of being. If you felt contradictory feelings or acted differently in different situations, that was seen as a problem to fix.

IFS flips this idea on its head. Dr. Schwartz discovered that everyone—yes, everyone—has multiple parts. The goal isn't to get rid of these parts or force them all to be the same. The goal is to help them work together better, like turning a dysfunctional family into a functional one.

Let me give you an example. Meet Marcus, a 28-year-old graphic designer:

Marcus wakes up Monday morning, and immediately different parts of him start talking:

Part 1 (anxious voice): "You have that big presentation today. What if you mess up? Everyone will think you're incompetent."

Part 2 (angry voice): "Why do we even care what they think? This job is stupid anyway. Maybe we should just quit."

Part 3 (reasonable voice): "Let's just get through the day. Make the presentation, do your best, go home."

Part 4 (young, scared voice): "I don't want to go. Remember in third grade when you forgot your lines in the school play? This feels like that."

All of these voices are parts of Marcus. None of them are "the real Marcus"—they're all real, and they're all trying to help him in their own way. The anxious part wants to prepare him for potential failure. The angry part wants to protect him from criticism. The reasonable part wants to get things done. The young part is remembering an old wound that still feels fresh.

How Richard Schwartz Discovered IFS

Dr. Schwartz didn't wake up one day and invent this idea out of nowhere. He discovered it by actually listening to his clients.

In the early 1980s, Schwartz was working as a family therapist. He specialized in helping people with eating disorders—things like bulimia and anorexia. He noticed something strange: his clients kept talking about themselves using language like "a part of me wants to eat" and "another part of me says I'm disgusting."

At first, he thought this was just a figure of speech. But the more he listened, the more he realized his clients were describing actual distinct parts of themselves, complete with different feelings, different ages, and different goals.

Schwartz had been trained in family systems therapy, where you look at how family members interact and affect each other. He had a lightbulb moment: what if he could apply those same principles to the internal "family" inside each person?

He started asking his clients to talk directly to these parts, to get to know them instead of fighting them. And something amazing happened—people started healing. Parts that had been causing problems for years suddenly relaxed when they felt understood. The eating disorders improved. The anxiety decreased. People felt more at peace with themselves.

How IFS Is Different from Other Therapies

If you've tried therapy before, IFS might feel different from what you're used to. Here's why:

Traditional therapy often focuses on analyzing your problems, understanding where they came from, and developing coping strategies. You might talk about your childhood, your relationships, your thought patterns.

Cognitive Behavioral Therapy (CBT) focuses on changing negative thought patterns and behaviors. If you think "I'm a failure,"

CBT helps you challenge that thought and replace it with something more realistic.

IFS does something unique: it asks you to actually get to know the parts of you that are struggling. Instead of trying to change your thoughts or analyze why you feel a certain way, IFS invites you to have a conversation with the part of you that's in pain.

Let me show you what I mean with an example:

Emma has terrible social anxiety. At parties, she freezes up, can't think of anything to say, and usually leaves early feeling like a failure.

In traditional talk therapy, Emma might explore where this anxiety came from. Maybe she'd remember being bullied in middle school. She'd understand the roots of her anxiety better.

In CBT, Emma would challenge her anxious thoughts. When her mind says "Everyone thinks you're boring," she'd counter with "That's not true. I have friends who enjoy talking to me."

In IFS, Emma would actually talk to the anxious part directly. She might ask it: "How old are you? What are you afraid of? What are you trying to protect me from?" She'd discover that this part is actually a 13-year-old version of herself that's still terrified of being rejected like she was in middle school. Instead of fighting this part or trying to logic it away, Emma would offer it compassion and understanding.

The difference is subtle but powerful. IFS treats your parts as legitimate members of your internal family who deserve to be heard, not as problems to be fixed.

Who Can Benefit from IFS Therapy?

Here's the short answer: pretty much everyone.

IFS was originally used to treat trauma, eating disorders, and addiction. But over the years, therapists discovered it works for just about any human struggle:

- **Anxiety and depression** – When you're stuck in cycles of worry or hopelessness
- **Relationship problems** – When you keep having the same fights or patterns with partners
- **Trauma and PTSD** – When past events still feel present and overwhelming
- **Addiction and compulsive behaviors** – When you can't stop doing something even though you want to
- **Low self-esteem** – When you're constantly criticizing yourself
- **Work stress and burnout** – When you feel pulled in too many directions
- **Life transitions** – When you're facing big changes and don't know who you are anymore

But here's what's really cool about IFS: you don't have to have a diagnosed problem to benefit from it. IFS can help anyone who wants to understand themselves better, make better decisions, or feel more at peace with who they are.

Think of it this way: everyone has an internal family. Some families are relatively calm and cooperative. Others are in constant chaos. IFS gives you tools to bring more harmony to your internal family, whatever shape it's in.

Real-Life IFS in Action

Let me introduce you to a few people and show you what IFS looks like in everyday life:

Carlos, 35, Software Engineer

Carlos is great at his job. He writes clean code, meets deadlines, and is respected by his team. But he has a secret: he hasn't taken a real vacation in four years. Every time he tries to plan time off, he gets this overwhelming sense that something bad will happen if he's not available. So he takes his laptop on "vacations" and checks his email constantly.

In IFS terms, Carlos has a strong Manager part that believes keeping everything under control is the only way to stay safe. This part probably developed years ago, maybe when Carlos was a kid and his family went through financial troubles. The Manager learned that being responsible and never slipping up was the key to survival.

But Carlos also has other parts. There's a tired part that's exhausted and needs rest. There's a playful part that wants to surf and hang out at the beach. There's a part that feels resentful about always working. These parts are in conflict with the Manager, creating internal stress.

With IFS, Carlos would learn to talk to his Manager part, understand where it came from, and help it see that it's okay to relax sometimes. The world won't fall apart if Carlos takes a week off.

Jasmine, 42, High School Teacher

Jasmine is known as the "nice teacher." Students love her because she's understanding and never gets mad. But here's the problem: Jasmine can't set boundaries. Students turn in work weeks late, and she accepts it. Colleagues dump extra duties on her, and she says yes. Her own kids complain she never has energy for them because she's exhausted from taking care of everyone else.

Jasmine has a People-Pleaser part that runs most of her life. This part believes that if Jasmine ever says no or disappoints someone, she'll be rejected and alone. Where did this part learn that? Probably from growing up with a parent who gave her love conditionally— only when she was "good" and helpful.

But Jasmine also has an angry part that's furious about being taken advantage of. And she has a part that feels empty and sad, like her own needs never matter. These parts are trying to get Jasmine's attention, but the People-Pleaser keeps pushing them down.

Through IFS, Jasmine would learn that the People-Pleaser is trying to protect her from an old fear that isn't as relevant anymore. She's an adult now, not a child dependent on her parents' approval. She can learn to set boundaries without being rejected.

Derek, 23, Recent College Graduate

Derek can't figure out what to do with his life. He graduated six months ago with a degree in business, but he hasn't applied for any jobs. Instead, he spends most of his time playing video games, scrolling social media, and feeling guilty about wasting time.

Derek has several parts in conflict. There's a part that wants to be successful and make his parents proud. There's a part that's terrified of failure and rejection (What if I apply for jobs and no one wants me?). There's a part that's still trying to figure out what Derek actually wants versus what everyone expects him to want. And there's a part that uses video games and phone scrolling to numb out from all this internal conflict.

These parts are pulling Derek in different directions, leaving him paralyzed. IFS would help Derek hear from each part, understand what they need, and find a way forward that honors all of them.

The Most Important Thing to Remember

Before we move on to the next chapter, I want you to remember this: IFS is not about getting rid of parts of yourself. It's not about fixing yourself or becoming someone different.

IFS is about getting to know all the parts of who you already are, understanding why they do what they do, and helping them work together better.

Think of yourself as the conductor of an orchestra. You don't get rid of the instruments you don't like. You don't force the violins to play like drums. Instead, you help each instrument play its part at the right time, creating beautiful music together.

In the next chapter, we'll talk about the conductor of your internal orchestra: your Core Self.

Chapter 2: Meet the Core Self - Your Inner Leader

Pop quiz: Who are you?

I don't mean your name or your job title. I mean who are you really, underneath all the roles you play and all the different ways you act?

Maybe you're thinking, "That's a weird question." Or maybe you're thinking, "I have no idea." Both responses make sense, because most of us have never really met our Core Self.

In IFS, the Self is not just another part. It's the essential you—the awareness that's experiencing everything, the "you" that's been there your whole life watching everything unfold. And here's the amazing thing: your Self can never be damaged.

What Is the Self in IFS?

Imagine you're watching a movie. There are all these characters on screen doing things, experiencing emotions, having conflicts. But you're sitting in the theater watching it all. You're not IN the movie; you're the awareness experiencing the movie.

Your Self is like that awareness. Your parts are like the characters in the movie—they have strong feelings, they react to situations, they try to solve problems. But your Self is the calm presence that can observe all of it without getting swept away.

Dr. Schwartz discovered something remarkable when working with his clients: when people were able to separate from their parts even a little bit, they naturally accessed qualities like compassion, curiosity, and calm. He didn't have to teach them to be compassionate. It just showed up automatically when parts stepped back.

This led him to a radical idea: maybe everyone has this wise, compassionate core already inside them. Maybe healing isn't about learning new skills or fixing what's broken. Maybe it's about removing the obstacles so the Self can lead.

Think of it like the sun. Even on the cloudiest day, the sun is still shining above the clouds. Your parts are like clouds—sometimes there are a lot of them, blocking the sun completely. But the sun never actually goes away. When the clouds part, even for a moment, there it is.

Your Self is always there, even when you can't feel it.

The 8 C's of Self-Energy

How do you know when you're in Self? Dr. Schwartz identified eight qualities that show up when the Self is present. He calls them the 8 C's:

1. Calm When you're in Self, you feel a sense of inner peace, even if the situation around you is chaotic. Your body relaxes. Your breathing slows down. You're not in fight-or-flight mode.

2. Clarity Your thinking is clear. You can see the situation for what it is, without the fog of strong emotions or old memories distorting your view.

3. Curiosity You're genuinely interested in understanding things. Instead of judging or reacting, you ask questions. You want to know more.

4. Compassion You feel care and concern, both for yourself and for others. You can recognize suffering and want to ease it.

5. Confidence Not arrogance—just a quiet sense that you can handle what comes. You trust yourself.

6. Courage You can face difficult things. You don't run away from fear; you move toward what matters even when it's scary.

7. Creativity You see new possibilities. You think outside the box. Solutions come more easily.

8. Connectedness You feel linked to something larger than yourself—to other people, to nature, to life itself. You're not alone or isolated.

Notice what's NOT on this list: anxiety, self-criticism, anger, shame, fear. Those come from parts, not from Self.

Let me show you what this looks like in real life:

Keisha's Two Responses

Keisha, a 31-year-old marketing manager, gets an email from her boss saying they need to talk tomorrow morning. No other context, just "Let's meet at 9am."

Response #1 - Coming from Parts: Keisha's stomach drops. Her anxious part immediately assumes she's in trouble: *Oh god, what did I do wrong? Is he firing me? Did I mess up the campaign?* Her mind races through every possible mistake. She can't focus on anything else for the rest of the day. She barely sleeps that night. By morning, she's rehearsed a dozen defensive explanations for mistakes she might have made.

Response #2 - Coming from Self: Keisha notices the email and feels a small flutter of anxiety. But instead of getting swept into the anxiety, she pauses. She takes a breath. She thinks: *I don't actually know what this is about. It could be anything—positive, negative, or neutral. I'll find out tomorrow.* She feels calm enough to keep working. That night, she acknowledges feeling a bit nervous, but she's not consumed by it. She sleeps fine. The next morning, she goes to the meeting with curiosity about what her boss wants to discuss.

What's the difference? In Response #1, Keisha's anxious part is running the show. In Response #2, Keisha's Self is present, able to notice the anxious part without being taken over by it.

(By the way, the meeting was about a promotion. The anxious part's catastrophizing was completely wrong.)

How to Recognize When You're in Self

Here's a simple test: when you're facing a situation, notice what's present in you.

Do you feel:

- Defensive?
- Judgmental?
- Overwhelmed?
- Numb or shut down?
- Panicked?
- Rageful?
- Desperate to fix it immediately?

If yes, you're probably in a part, not in Self.

Do you feel:

- Spacious inside, like you have room to breathe?
- Curious about what's happening?
- Open to different outcomes?
- Connected to your body in a grounded way?
- Able to see the bigger picture?
- Compassionate toward everyone involved, including yourself?

If yes, you're probably in Self, or at least closer to it.

Let's look at another example:

Antonio and His Teenager

Antonio's 16-year-old daughter, Maya, comes home two hours past curfew. She won't say where she was. She's defensive and dismissive.

Antonio in Parts: His angry part explodes: "You're grounded for a month! I can't believe you'd be so irresponsible!" His anxious part is terrified something bad happened or will happen. His own teenage part remembers getting in trouble with his strict father and feels that same rebellious energy. His authoritarian part thinks if he doesn't crack down hard, Maya will keep pushing boundaries. All these parts are fighting for control, and Antonio ends up yelling things he'll regret later.

Antonio in Self: Antonio feels angry and worried—those feelings are valid. But he's not taken over by them. He takes a breath and says, "I was really worried about you. I need to understand what happened, and we need to talk about curfew. But right now, I can see you're upset, and I'm upset too. Let's both cool down and talk in the morning when we can actually hear each other." He goes to bed troubled but not consumed. The next day, he has a real conversation with Maya, where he listens to her perspective and explains his concerns. They work out a solution together.

The Self doesn't mean you don't have feelings. It means you're not hijacked by them.

What Happens When Parts Take Over the Self

In IFS language, when a part takes over, we call it "blending." The part blends with the Self so completely that you can't tell the difference anymore. You don't think "A part of me is scared." You think "I am scared" or even just feel scared without any awareness that it's a part.

Think of it like trying to drive a car while someone else keeps grabbing the steering wheel. Your Self is supposed to be driving—

making decisions, navigating life. But when parts blend, they grab the wheel and suddenly you're swerving all over the road.

Here are some signs that parts have blended with your Self:

Time Travel: You're not in the present moment. You're reliving the past or catastrophizing about the future.

All-or-Nothing Thinking: Everything is black and white, good or bad, safe or dangerous. You've lost the ability to see nuance.

Reactive Behavior: You do things on impulse that you later regret—send angry texts, make big decisions hastily, say things you don't mean.

Physical Tension: Your body is tight, your breathing is shallow, your heart is racing or your chest feels heavy.

Loss of Perspective: Whatever the part is focused on feels like the only thing that matters. You can't zoom out and see the bigger picture.

Let me show you what this looks like:

Nina's Job Interview

Nina has a job interview for a position she really wants. As the interview approaches, her parts start blending:

Week Before: A perfectionist part blends. Nina can't think about anything except the interview. She practices answers for hours. She researches the company obsessively. She loses sleep thinking about potential questions.

Day Before: An anxious part blends even more. Nina's stomach hurts. She keeps thinking *I'm going to blow this. I never interview well. Why did I even apply?* She considers canceling.

Interview Day: As Nina sits in the waiting room, a young part blends—the part of her that's still the awkward middle schooler who never felt good enough. Her hands shake. Her voice comes out small and uncertain. She gives answers she's practiced, but they sound robotic.

After Interview: A critical part blends. *You idiot. You totally messed that up. They probably laughed after you left. You'll never get hired anywhere.*

At no point during this whole experience was Nina's Self in charge. Different parts kept grabbing the steering wheel, and Nina got yanked around by all of them.

Now let's imagine Nina with her Self more present:

Week Before: Nina notices she's feeling anxious about the interview. She talks to that anxious part: *I hear you. You want me to be prepared. That makes sense. Let's prepare reasonably without going overboard.* She practices a bit but also makes sure to do things she enjoys to stay balanced.

Day Before: The anxiety intensifies. Nina sits with it for a moment. *Part of me is really scared. That's okay. I've been scared before and gotten through it.* She does something grounding—takes a walk, calls a friend, takes a bath.

Interview Day: Nina feels nervous energy as she waits, but she's not consumed by it. She reminds herself: *I'm qualified for this. They chose to interview me for a reason. I'll do my best and see what happens.* During the interview, she's present, listening to the questions, responding authentically.

After Interview: Nina feels that familiar self-critical voice start up, but she catches it. *Hey, critical part, I see you. You're trying to protect me from disappointment by beating me to the punch. But actually, I think I did okay. Some answers were great, some were* *just fine. That's normal.* She's able to let go and wait for the response.

The difference is night and day, right? And it all comes from having the Self more present.

Why Your Self Can Never Be Damaged

This is one of the most hopeful ideas in IFS: no matter what you've been through, your Self is still there, intact and whole.

You might have parts that are deeply wounded. You might have parts that are scared, ashamed, or enraged. You might have parts that do destructive things. But underneath all of that, your Self remains undamaged.

Think about this: Have you ever had a moment, even in the middle of a terrible situation, where you suddenly felt strangely calm? Where you could see clearly what needed to happen? Where you felt connected to something larger than your immediate pain?

That was your Self, breaking through the clouds.

Miguel's Story

Miguel grew up in a chaotic home. His father had a drinking problem and would get violent when drunk. His mother was checked out, overwhelmed, unable to protect Miguel and his siblings. By the time Miguel was 10, he felt like he had to be the adult in the family—making sure his little brother got to school, hiding when dad came home drunk, managing his own emotions so he wouldn't add to the chaos.

Miguel developed a lot of protective parts. A hypervigilant part that was always scanning for danger. A controlling part that tried to manage every situation. A part that shut down his own needs because they weren't safe to have. A part that raged when he finally moved out and didn't have to be so controlled anymore.

18

By the time Miguel was 30, he had a good job and lived far from his family, but he was miserable. He had panic attacks. He couldn't maintain relationships because he either tried to control everything or exploded in anger. He felt broken.

When Miguel started IFS therapy, he discovered something shocking: underneath all those protective parts, underneath all that pain, there was a part of him that had never been damaged.

His Self was still there.

It had been there when he was 10, quietly doing what needed to be done to survive. It had been there in his 20s when he finally got away and started building a life. It was there now, ready to help him heal.

Miguel's parts were wounded. His parts were exhausted. His parts were doing extreme things to cope. But his Self? His Self was fine. It was just buried under a lot of protective parts.

The work wasn't about creating a new, better Miguel. It was about helping his parts relax enough so the Miguel that had always been there could finally lead his life.

Accessing Your Self

So how do you access this Self? How do you get to it when it feels buried under a mountain of anxious, critical, or angry parts?

The good news: you don't have to work hard to create Self-energy. You just have to help the parts step back a little.

In IFS, we call this "unblending." You ask the parts to give you some space. Not to go away—just to separate from you enough that you can be in the Self.

Here's a simple way to try it:

The Pause Practice

1. Notice when you're feeling a strong emotion or having a strong reaction.
2. Take a breath and ask internally: *What part of me is feeling this?*
3. See if you can get a sense of the part. Where is it in your body? What does it look like? How old does it seem?
4. Ask the part: *Would you be willing to give me a little space? You can stay close, but just separate from me a bit so I can talk to you.*
5. Notice what happens. Do you feel any sense of space opening up? Do you feel any of those C-qualities emerging—calm, curiosity, compassion?
6. From that place of more space, ask the part: *What do you want me to know?*

Let's see this in practice:

Gabriela's Morning

Gabriela wakes up and immediately feels heavy dread. She doesn't want to get out of bed. She doesn't want to go to work. She doesn't want to do anything. In the past, she would have either forced herself through the day while feeling miserable, or called in sick and felt guilty about it.

But Gabriela has been learning IFS. So she tries something different:

What part of me is feeling this?

She gets an image of a small, tired child curled up in a ball.

Would you be willing to separate from me just a bit? You can stay here, but give me a little space?

She feels the heavy weight lift slightly. Not completely, but enough that she can breathe.

From this slightly more spacious place, Gabriela asks: *What do you want me to know?*

And the answer comes clearly: *I'm so tired. We never rest. It's just work, chores, obligations, over and over. I need a break.*

Gabriela feels compassion for this exhausted part. She's in her Self now—she can feel it. She responds: *You're right. We've been pushing really hard. I hear you. Let me think about what we can do.*

She still goes to work that day, but she makes a decision: she's going to take a real day off this weekend. No errands, no obligations, just rest. And she makes a plan to talk to her boss about adjusting her schedule.

The exhausted part relaxes a bit, just from being heard.

This is the Self in action: hearing the part, taking it seriously, and responding with wisdom and compassion.

Living from the Self

Here's what I want you to understand: the goal of IFS isn't to be in your Self 100% of the time. That's not realistic, and it's not even the goal.

The goal is to have your Self accessible enough that it can lead. To have enough space between you and your parts that you can choose how to respond instead of being hijacked by reactions.

Think of it like parenting. Good parents don't ignore their children's feelings or needs. They listen, they care, they respond. But they don't let the three-year-old make all the decisions about what the family does.

Your Self is like a good parent to your parts. It listens to them, cares about them, takes their needs seriously—but it makes the final decisions about how you'll live your life.

21

In the next chapter, we'll start meeting some of your parts more specifically. We'll begin with the parts that are most often in charge: the Managers.

Chapter 3: Understanding Your Protector Parts - The Managers

Let's start with a question: What's the first thing you do when you wake up in the morning?

Maybe you check your phone. Maybe you start running through your to-do list. Maybe you immediately start worrying about everything you need to get done. Maybe you lie there thinking about something you said yesterday that might have come across wrong.

If any of this sounds familiar, you've just met your Manager parts.

What Are Manager Parts?

Manager parts are the organizers, planners, and preventers of your internal family. Their job is to make sure nothing bad happens. They try to control your environment, your behavior, and even your emotions to keep you safe from pain, rejection, failure, or any other kind of hurt.

Think of Managers like the responsible older sibling who's constantly making sure everyone in the family is behaving correctly so the parents don't get mad. Managers learned at some point in your life that if they stay on top of things, if they keep everything under control, bad things won't happen.

The problem? Managers tend to be exhausted overachievers who can never quite relax, because staying safe means staying vigilant.

Here's the key thing to understand: Manager parts aren't trying to make your life miserable. They're trying to protect you. Everything they do, even the stuff that makes you unhappy, comes from a positive intention to keep you safe.

How Managers Try to Keep You Safe

Managers have lots of strategies for keeping you safe. Let's look at some of the most common approaches:

Prevention: Managers try to prevent bad things before they happen. If you might fail, don't try. If you might be rejected, don't put yourself out there. If you might look stupid, stay quiet.

Control: Managers try to control everything they possibly can. Plan every detail. Make sure nothing unexpected happens. Keep your environment predictable.

Performance: Managers push you to be perfect, successful, or impressive so nobody can criticize you or reject you.

Caretaking: Managers make you focus on everyone else's needs so people won't abandon you or get mad at you.

Distraction: Managers keep you busy with tasks and productivity so you don't have time to feel painful emotions.

All of these strategies share a common goal: keep the bad stuff from happening. Keep the painful feelings away. Stay safe.

Let's meet some specific Manager parts:

The Perfectionist

Meet Tyler, 27, Architect

Tyler spends hours on every project, tweaking tiny details that probably nobody else will notice. He revises his work emails five times before sending them. When he makes dinner for friends, he's so stressed about getting everything right that he barely enjoys the evening. He exercises exactly six times a week, meal preps every Sunday, and keeps his apartment spotlessly clean.

Tyler's Perfectionist Manager believes that if everything is perfect, he'll be safe from criticism. Where did this part learn that?

When Tyler was eight, his dad would criticize him for small mistakes. If Tyler got a 95 on a test, his dad would ask why it wasn't a 100. If Tyler cleaned his room but forgot to organize his bookshelf, his dad would point out what he missed instead of acknowledging what he'd done. Young Tyler learned: Perfect = Safe. Anything less than perfect = Criticism and disappointment.

Now Tyler is an adult. His dad's opinion isn't the most important thing in his life anymore. But his Perfectionist Manager is still running the same old program, trying to protect him from criticism that might not even come.

The exhausting part? Perfection is impossible. So Tyler's Perfectionist is always working, always stressed, never satisfied.

The Perfectionist's Positive Intention: To protect you from criticism, rejection, or the feeling of not being good enough.

The People-Pleaser

Meet Rachel, 34, Social Worker

Rachel has a hard time saying no. When her friend asks her to help move on her only day off, Rachel says yes even though she's exhausted. When her colleague asks her to cover a shift, she agrees even though she already has plans. When her partner suggests a restaurant Rachel doesn't like, she goes along with it without mentioning her preference.

Rachel's People-Pleaser Manager monitors everyone else's emotions constantly. Is that person mad at me? Did I disappoint them? Do they still like me? The People-Pleaser works overtime to keep everyone happy, because somewhere deep inside, Rachel believes that if she disappoints people, they'll leave.

Where did Rachel's People-Pleaser learn this?

Rachel's mom struggled with depression. As a kid, Rachel learned that her mom was happiest when Rachel was being easy and agreeable. If Rachel expressed needs or complained, her mom would withdraw into sadness. Child Rachel couldn't handle losing her mom's presence like that, so she learned to push her own needs aside and focus on keeping mom happy.

The People-Pleaser worked brilliantly back then. But now Rachel is depleted. She doesn't know what she actually wants anymore because she's spent so long focusing on what everyone else wants.

The People-Pleaser's Positive Intention: To protect you from abandonment, rejection, or being alone.

The Planner

Meet Jordan, 29, Freelance Writer

Jordan has lists for everything. To-do lists, goal lists, grocery lists, lists of lists. He plans his day in 30-minute increments. He researches vacation destinations for months before booking. He has backup plans for his backup plans.

Jordan's Planner Manager believes that if everything is mapped out, nothing can go wrong. If Jordan anticipates every possibility and prepares for it, he'll be in control.

But here's what actually happens: Jordan's Planner makes him so focused on the future that he misses the present. He's always thinking three steps ahead instead of experiencing what's happening right now. And when something unexpected happens—which it always does—Jordan feels anxious and thrown off.

Jordan's Planner developed when he was 12 and his parents went through a messy divorce. Everything in Jordan's life felt chaotic and unpredictable. His Planner part stepped up and said, "I'll make things predictable. I'll control what I can control." It helped Jordan survive a difficult time.

But now? Jordan's life is relatively stable, but his Planner is still in emergency mode, trying to control things that don't need to be controlled.

The Planner's Positive Intention: To protect you from chaos, surprises, and feeling out of control.

The Inner Critic

Meet Vanessa, 31, Teacher

There's a voice in Vanessa's head that never shuts up. It comments on everything:

That was a stupid thing to say. You look terrible in that outfit. Everyone else is doing better than you. Why can't you be more organized/disciplined/successful?

Vanessa's Inner Critic is relentless. It attacks her constantly, pointing out every flaw, every mistake, every way she falls short of where she "should" be.

Here's what most people don't understand about the Inner Critic: it's actually trying to help.

The Critic believes that if it criticizes you first, you'll improve yourself before anyone else can judge you. It's like a brutal coach who thinks harsh words will make you perform better. The Critic is trying to make you so perfect that nobody can hurt you.

Vanessa's Inner Critic developed when she was bullied in middle school. Girls would mock her appearance, her interests, her quirks. The bullying was terrible. But you know what was worse? Not seeing it coming. Being surprised by the attacks.

So Vanessa's Critic stepped in and started attacking her first. *If I point out all my flaws before anyone else can, I won't be caught off guard. I can fix them. I can be ready.*

The tragedy is that Vanessa's Critic is harsher than any bully ever was. It never takes a day off. And no matter what Vanessa achieves, the Critic finds something wrong.

The Inner Critic's Positive Intention: To protect you from criticism and rejection by making you "better" before anyone can judge you.

The Worrier

Meet Kevin, 38, Small Business Owner

Kevin's brain runs worst-case scenarios 24/7.

What if the business fails? What if I can't make payroll? What if that pain in my chest is a heart attack? What if my wife leaves me? What if my kids end up resenting me? What if I'm making a huge mistake? What if, what if, what if?

Kevin's Worrier Manager is trying to keep him safe by anticipating every possible danger. If Kevin thinks about what could go wrong, the Worrier believes, he can prepare for it or prevent it.

The problem is that 99% of the things Kevin worries about never happen. But his Worrier doesn't care about statistics. Its job is to scan for threats, and in our modern world, there are infinite things to worry about.

Kevin's Worrier got intense after his brother died in a car accident when Kevin was 22. The death came out of nowhere—totally unexpected. Kevin's world shattered. His Worrier part came online in full force, determined to never be caught off guard again.

If I worry about it, maybe I can prevent it. If I anticipate it, at least I won't be blindsided like I was when my brother died.

Of course, worry doesn't actually prevent bad things. But Kevin's Worrier doesn't know that. It just keeps working, exhausting Kevin in the process.

The Worrier's Positive Intention: To protect you from being caught off guard by bad things.

Why Managers Work Overtime

Here's the pattern you probably noticed: all these Manager parts developed in response to something. They learned their strategies when you were younger, often in response to pain, fear, or instability.

And here's the thing: those strategies probably worked back then. The Perfectionist helped you avoid your dad's criticism. The People-Pleaser helped you stay connected to your mom. The Planner helped you feel safe during the divorce. The Inner Critic helped you armor up against bullies. The Worrier tried to prevent another devastating surprise.

Your Managers aren't stupid. They're not broken. They developed smart strategies to protect you during difficult times.

The problem is that Managers don't always update their strategies when circumstances change. They keep running the same old programs even when you're not in danger anymore.

It's like having a security system that was installed in a high-crime neighborhood, but you've since moved to a safe suburb. The alarm still goes off at every little noise because it's calibrated for a level of danger that no longer exists.

The Cost of Manager Control

When Managers are running your life, there are costs:

Exhaustion: Managers never stop working. Constant vigilance, constant effort, constant control. It's tiring.

Anxiety: When Managers are in charge, you're always bracing for something bad. You can't relax.

Rigidity: Managers like things a certain way. They don't handle change or spontaneity well.

Disconnection: When you're in Manager mode, you're in your head—planning, criticizing, controlling. You're not present with what's actually happening.

Lost Authenticity: Managers often make you behave in ways that get approval but aren't actually you. You lose touch with what you really want or feel.

Let me show you what this looks like:

Briana's Weekend

Briana is excited about a weekend getaway with friends. She's been looking forward to it for weeks.

But as the weekend approaches, her Managers kick into high gear:

Her **Perfectionist** starts worrying about what to pack. She revises her packing list multiple times. She googles the weather obsessively.

Her **People-Pleaser** starts managing everyone else's experience. She texts the group suggesting activities, making sure everyone's happy with the plans, trying to anticipate conflicts.

Her **Planner** creates an itinerary. She researches restaurants, makes reservations, maps out driving routes.

Her **Inner Critic** starts commenting on her appearance. She tries on multiple outfits, dissatisfied with all of them. *You need to lose weight before this trip. Everyone else will look better than you.*

Her **Worrier** spins catastrophic scenarios. *What if someone gets sick? What if we get in an accident? What if the cabin is terrible? What if you all run out of things to talk about and it gets awkward?*

By the time Briana gets to the weekend, she's already exhausted. Her Managers have been working so hard that there's no room for her Self to actually enjoy the experience. She spends the weekend in her head—managing, monitoring, controlling—instead of just being present with her friends.

The weekend that was supposed to be fun and relaxing becomes another thing her Managers have to manage.

Working with Managers

Here's what you need to understand: you don't want to get rid of your Managers. They're trying to help. They care about you. They've been working hard to keep you safe.

What you want is to help them relax a bit. To update their strategies. To let your Self lead instead of having them run the whole show.

In IFS, we do this by actually talking to the Manager parts. Not fighting them or trying to logic them away—actually having a conversation.

Here's what that might look like:

Diego and His Perfectionist

Diego has been trying to finish a proposal for work. His Perfectionist has made him rewrite it six times. It's 2am, and Diego is exhausted and frustrated.

31

Instead of just pushing through (which is what he usually does), Diego tries something different. He pauses and says internally:

Hey, Perfectionist part. I know you're trying to help here. Can you tell me what you're worried about?

He gets a clear sense of the answer: *If this proposal isn't perfect, they'll think you're incompetent. You'll lose credibility. You might lose your job.*

Okay, I hear you. That sounds really scary. When did you start worrying about this?

An image comes to Diego's mind: he's in high school, working on a big project. He turned it in thinking it was good, but he got a C. The teacher wrote harsh comments all over it. Diego felt humiliated.

Got it. You learned that if work isn't perfect, I'll be humiliated. That makes sense. That was a painful experience.

Diego feels compassion for this part of him that's still trying to prevent that humiliation.

Here's the thing, though. I'm not in high school anymore. I'm good at my job. This proposal is solid—I've checked it with two colleagues already. It doesn't need to be perfect. It needs to be good enough. And it already is.

But what if— the Perfectionist starts.

I know you're scared. But I've got this. I'm going to submit the proposal as it is. You can take a break. I'll handle whatever response comes.

Diego feels the Perfectionist relax just a bit. Enough that he can submit the proposal and go to bed.

That's what working with Managers looks like. Not fighting them. Not ignoring them. Actually hearing their fears and helping them see that the Self can handle things now.

Recognizing Your Own Managers

Before we move on, take a moment to think about your own Manager parts. What strategies do they use to keep you safe?

Do you have a Perfectionist who makes everything need to be just right?

A People-Pleaser who can't say no?

A Planner who needs to control every detail?

An Inner Critic who attacks you constantly?

A Worrier who catastrophizes about everything?

Maybe you have all of these. Maybe you have different ones I haven't mentioned.

The important thing is to start noticing them. Not to judge them or try to make them go away—just to see them and recognize that they're trying to help, even when their help feels more like a burden.

In the next chapter, we'll meet a different type of part: the ones your Managers are working so hard to protect you from. We'll meet the Exiles.

Chapter 4: The Wounded Parts - Your Exiles

Have you ever had a moment where something small happened—someone canceled plans, you made a tiny mistake at work, someone said something mildly critical—and suddenly you felt completely devastated? Like, way more upset than the situation warranted?

Maybe you felt like a worthless failure over a minor error. Maybe you felt totally abandoned because a friend rescheduled. Maybe you felt deep shame over something that was barely your fault.

If this has happened to you, you've just gotten a glimpse of your Exile parts.

What Are Exile Parts?

Exiles are the parts of you that carry old wounds. They hold the pain, fear, shame, and trauma from your past—often from childhood, but not always. These parts got hurt at some point, and they're still stuck in that hurt, even though years or decades have passed.

They're called Exiles because they've been pushed away, locked up, hidden in the basement of your internal house. Why? Because what they carry is too painful. The feelings are too big, too overwhelming, too scary. So your protective parts (the Managers and, as we'll see in the next chapter, the Firefighters) work hard to keep these Exiles locked away where you don't have to feel what they feel.

Think of it like this: Imagine something terrible happened to a family member years ago. It was so painful that the family decided to never talk about it. That family member still carries the pain, but everyone pretends it's not there. They don't invite that person to family gatherings. They change the subject if they come up. They've essentially exiled them from the family.

That's what happens with Exile parts. They carry pain that felt too big to handle, so they got shut away. But just like a real person who's been excluded, these parts are still there, still hurting, still trying to get attention.

How Exiles Carry Pain and Trauma

Exiles typically carry what IFS calls "burdens." These are the painful beliefs and feelings they absorbed during difficult experiences:

Common Burdens Exiles Carry:

- Worthlessness: "I'm not good enough. I'm defective. There's something wrong with me."
- Shame: "I'm bad. I'm disgusting. I should be hidden."
- Terror: "The world isn't safe. Something terrible will happen."
- Abandonment: "Nobody wants me. I'll always be alone."
- Helplessness: "I can't handle things. I'm powerless."
- Unlovability: "I'm not worthy of love. Nobody will ever truly love me."

Here's what you need to understand: these aren't just thoughts. For Exiles, these feel like absolute truths. And often, these parts are frozen at the age when the original hurt happened.

Let me introduce you to some Exiles:

Liam's Seven-Year-Old Exile

Liam is 35 now, a successful software developer with a caring partner and good friends. But sometimes, out of nowhere, he feels absolutely certain that everyone secretly thinks he's stupid and is just being polite to him.

Where does this come from?

In IFS therapy, Liam discovered an Exile part that's seven years old. This part carries a memory from second grade: Liam was excited to share something in class. He misunderstood the assignment and said something that didn't make sense. The teacher corrected him, and several kids laughed. Liam felt stupid, humiliated, and small.

That seven-year-old part of Liam never fully processed that moment. He got stuck there, holding the belief "I'm stupid. People will laugh at me." The adult Liam knows intellectually that he's smart—he has a computer science degree, he solves complex problems every day. But when that Exile gets triggered, adult logic doesn't matter. The seven-year-old's pain floods Liam's system, and suddenly he's back in that classroom, feeling humiliated.

This is what Exiles do: they hold time capsules of pain that can get opened unexpectedly, making you feel things that don't match your current reality.

Why These Parts Get "Exiled"

Why would we push away parts of ourselves? Because children (and sometimes adults) can only handle so much pain at once.

Imagine you're eight years old. Something bad happens—maybe your parents are fighting constantly, or a parent is depressed and unavailable, or you're being bullied, or you experience something actually traumatic like abuse or a scary accident.

The feelings that come with these experiences are huge: terror, grief, rage, shame, helplessness. They're so big they feel like they might swallow you whole. Eight-year-old you can't process feelings that size. You don't have the tools, the support, or the safety to feel them fully and move through them.

So what happens? Your protective parts step in and say, "We need to lock this away. We need to make sure you don't feel this, because if you feel it, it will destroy you."

They push the wounded part down, away, into exile. And then the Managers work really hard to make sure that part stays there—because if it comes up, you'll have to feel all that pain.

Meredith's Story: Creating an Exile

Meredith is 40 now, but she has an Exile part that's frozen at age 11.

When Meredith was 11, her mom was diagnosed with cancer. The adults around Meredith didn't talk to her much about it. They said things like "Mom's going to be fine" and "Don't worry." But Meredith could see her mom was very sick. She was terrified.

Eleven-year-old Meredith felt overwhelming fear that her mom would die. She felt guilty for being scared (because the adults said not to worry). She felt lonely (because nobody talked to her about what was happening). She felt helpless (because she couldn't do anything to help her mom).

These feelings were too much for an 11-year-old to carry. So they got exiled. Manager parts stepped in to keep Meredith functioning: a part that acted cheerful and normal at school, a part that tried to be helpful and not add stress at home, a part that distracted her with homework and books.

Meredith's mom survived the cancer. But that 11-year-old part never got to process the terror and helplessness she felt. That part is still stuck in 2001, still scared, still alone with feelings that were too big.

Now, decades later, whenever someone Meredith loves gets sick—even with something minor like a cold—she has panic attacks. The Exile's terror comes flooding back, and adult Meredith is suddenly feeling the overwhelming fear of 11-year-old Meredith.

How Exiles Show Up in Adult Life

You might be thinking, "Okay, but I'm an adult now. Shouldn't I be over childhood stuff?"

Here's the thing: intellectual knowing doesn't change emotional wounds. You can understand logically that you're not that helpless child anymore, but the Exile part doesn't know that. It's still back there, still hurting.

Exiles show up in surprising ways:

Overreactions to Small Things: Cameron gets slightly critical feedback at work—his boss says his presentation could have been more concise—and Cameron feels absolutely crushed. He can barely function for the rest of the day. The feedback was mild, but it triggered an Exile that carries a belief that he's never good enough.

Intense Fear of Abandonment: Whitney's boyfriend says he needs some alone time this weekend. Whitney's rational mind understands that people need space. But she's flooded with panic: *He's going to leave me. I'm too much. He doesn't really love me.* An Exile that was abandoned by a parent is getting triggered, convinced the abandonment is happening again.

Shame Spirals: Jackson makes a mistake—he accidentally double-books himself and has to cancel plans with a friend. He feels overwhelming shame, like he's a terrible person. He beats himself up for hours, imagining that his friend hates him now. A small mistake has triggered an Exile that carries deep shame.

Physical Symptoms: Andrea feels nauseated and gets a headache whenever she has to visit her parents. She doesn't understand why—nothing bad happens at these visits. But her body is responding to an Exile that holds unprocessed feelings about her childhood, feelings she's never let herself fully acknowledge.

The Burdens Exiles Hold

Let's talk more specifically about what Exiles carry. In IFS, we call these "burdens"—the painful beliefs and feelings that parts absorbed during difficult experiences.

Imagine a backpack filled with heavy rocks. Each rock has a label: "I'm worthless." "I'm bad." "I'm unlovable." "The world is dangerous." "I'll always be alone." The Exile has been carrying this backpack since the original wound happened, and the weight is exhausting.

The beautiful thing about IFS is that these burdens don't have to be carried forever. Parts can unburden—they can put down the backpack and discover who they'd be without that weight. But we'll get to that process later. First, you need to understand what burdens your Exiles are carrying.

Common Burdens and Where They Come From:

"I'm not good enough" This burden often develops when love or approval was conditional. Maybe you only got attention when you achieved something. Maybe nothing you did was ever quite right. A part of you absorbed the message that your inherent value wasn't enough—you had to perform, achieve, or be perfect to be worthy.

Example: Zoe's parents both had demanding careers. They came to her school events and praised her achievements, but they were often distracted or stressed. Zoe learned that she got their attention and warm presence when she excelled at something. A part of her absorbed the burden: *I'm only valuable when I'm accomplishing things.*

"I'm bad/shameful" This burden comes from experiences where you felt like you were wrong at your core. Maybe you were blamed for things that weren't your fault. Maybe you were shamed for natural aspects of being human—having needs, making mistakes, expressing feelings.

Example: Marcus grew up in a religious household where normal childhood mistakes were treated as moral failures. If he talked back, it wasn't just misbehavior—it was "disrespecting God's order." If he struggled with sexual feelings as a teenager, it was sinful. A part of Marcus absorbed the burden: *There's something fundamentally bad in me.*

"I'm unlovable" This burden develops when love felt uncertain or conditional. Maybe a parent was emotionally unavailable. Maybe you were neglected or abandoned. Maybe you were rejected by peers during crucial developmental years.

Example: Elena's father left when she was five and barely stayed in touch after that. Her mom, overwhelmed and grieving, was emotionally distant. Elena didn't understand why her dad left or why her mom seemed so far away. A five-year-old doesn't think, "My parents are dealing with their own issues." She thinks, *There must be something wrong with me. If I was lovable, Dad would have stayed. If I was lovable, Mom would be warmer.*

"The world isn't safe" This burden comes from experiences of actual danger, chaos, or unpredictability. Maybe you experienced abuse or violence. Maybe your home was unstable. Maybe something scary happened that shattered your sense of security.

Example: Jamal was in a serious car accident when he was 16. He survived with minor injuries, but he was terrified. For weeks after, he had nightmares and panic attacks. His family wanted him to "get over it" and go back to normal, so Jamal pushed the fear away. But a part of him still holds that terror, still believes *Danger can come out of nowhere. The world isn't safe.*

Understanding Childhood Wounds in Adult Life

Here's something important: not all wounds come from obvious trauma. Sometimes Exiles develop from experiences that look minor from the outside but felt huge to the child experiencing them.

Maybe your parents were basically good, but they were stressed and overwhelmed. They didn't have much bandwidth for your feelings. You learned to push your emotions down.

Maybe you had one really humiliating experience with peers that taught you being vulnerable isn't safe.

Maybe your family was overall loving, but there was one area where you felt unseen or misunderstood.

These experiences can create Exiles too. IFS isn't about blaming your parents or past experiences. It's about recognizing that parts of you got hurt and still carry that hurt, regardless of whether the original situation was "bad enough" to justify it.

Trevor's "Small" Wound

Trevor had a pretty good childhood. His parents loved him, he had friends, nothing obviously traumatic happened. But Trevor's dad was a stoic, "tough it out" kind of guy who believed boys shouldn't cry or be "too sensitive."

When Trevor was nine, his dog died—his best friend since he was four. Trevor was devastated. He cried in his room. His dad came in and said, "Come on, buddy. It's sad, but you need to be strong. Don't let this knock you down."

His dad meant well. He wanted to help Trevor cope. But what nine-year-old Trevor heard was: *My sadness is too much. I need to be strong instead of feeling this.*

From that moment, Trevor learned to exile his grief. Whenever he felt sad, a Manager part would step in and push it away: *Don't be weak. Just get over it.*

Now Trevor is 32. He hasn't cried in 15 years. He prides himself on being strong and rational. But he also feels numb a lot of the time.

41

He has trouble connecting deeply with people. And sometimes, for no clear reason, he feels this heavy sadness he can't explain.

That's his nine-year-old Exile, still carrying the grief he never got to fully feel.

Why Protectors Work So Hard to Keep Exiles Away

Here's the pattern: something painful happened. An Exile part formed around that pain. Protective parts (Managers and Firefighters) stepped in to make sure you never have to feel that pain again.

Your Managers use preventive strategies: stay in control, be perfect, keep everyone happy, plan everything, criticize yourself before others can. If the Managers can keep life stable and predictable, the Exiles won't get triggered.

But sometimes, despite the Managers' best efforts, life happens. Something triggers an Exile. The feelings start coming up. The pain threatens to break through.

That's when Firefighters show up—but we'll talk about them in the next chapter.

For now, what you need to understand is why your protective parts are so intense: they're protecting you from Exiles that carry enormous pain.

Think about it: if you have an Exile that holds a belief like "I'm completely worthless," and that Exile gets triggered, you don't just think "I'm worthless" like an abstract thought. You feel it like the truth of your entire existence. The pain is overwhelming.

Your protective parts know this. They've been doing their job— keeping you away from that pain—for years, maybe decades. They're not going to let you access those Exiles easily, because they think feeling that pain will destroy you.

This is why healing work with Exiles has to be done carefully, with the protective parts on board. You can't just bulldoze past the Managers and Firefighters to get to the Exiles. That would activate the protectors even more and could actually make things worse.

Acknowledging Your Exiles (Gently)

I want to be clear: this chapter isn't asking you to dive into your deepest wounds right now. That would be neither safe nor helpful without the right support and preparation.

What I am asking you to do is acknowledge that these wounded parts exist. To recognize that some of your intense reactions might be coming from parts that are still carrying old pain.

When you overreact to something small, instead of just feeling bad about overreacting, you might pause and think: *What part of me got triggered just now? What old wound does this touch?*

You don't have to fix it. You don't have to feel all the feelings right now. Just notice: *Oh, there's a hurt part here.*

A Gentle Exercise:

Think of a time recently when you had a strong emotional reaction that felt bigger than the situation warranted. Maybe you felt disproportionately hurt, scared, angry, or ashamed about something relatively small.

Now ask yourself:

- How old might the part be that felt those feelings?
- What might this part believe about you, others, or the world?
- What might this part be trying to tell you?

Don't try to fix or change anything. Just notice. Just acknowledge that there's a young, wounded part of you that's still hurting.

This is the beginning of healing: seeing the Exiles, recognizing they're there, and understanding that your protective parts have been working so hard to keep you away from that pain.

In the next chapter, we'll talk about what happens when the protective parts fail to keep the Exiles locked away. We'll meet the Firefighters—the emergency responders of your internal system.

Chapter 5: Emergency Responders - The Firefighters

Remember in the last chapter when we talked about how Managers work hard to keep Exiles locked away? Well, Managers aren't perfect. Sometimes, despite their best efforts, an Exile breaks through. The feelings start flooding in—the fear, the shame, the pain—and it feels unbearable.

That's when the Firefighters show up.

What Are Firefighter Parts?

Firefighters are the emergency responders of your internal system. When there's a fire—when an Exile's pain breaks through—Firefighters rush in with one goal: put out the fire NOW. They don't care about long-term consequences. They don't care if their methods cause other problems. They just need to stop the pain immediately.

Think of an actual firefighter responding to a house fire. They're not worried about the water damage they're causing or the broken windows. They're focused on one thing: put out the fire before it burns everything down. They'll do whatever it takes.

Your Firefighter parts work the same way. When emotional pain threatens to overwhelm you, they use whatever methods they can to shut it down fast.

The problem? Firefighter strategies often create more problems in the long run, even though they provide immediate relief.

How Firefighters React When Exiles Break Through

Firefighters use distraction, numbing, and impulsive behaviors to pull your attention away from the pain. Here are some of their favorite strategies:

Substance Use: Alcohol, drugs, prescription medication—anything that numbs feelings fast.

Overeating or Restricting: Bingeing to numb out, or restricting to feel control.

Excessive Shopping or Spending: The high of buying something new distracts from pain.

Compulsive Social Media or Internet Use: Endless scrolling keeps you from feeling.

Rage and Aggression: Anger feels more powerful than hurt or fear, so Firefighters blast rage to cover vulnerable feelings.

Self-Harm: Physical pain can override emotional pain.

Risky or Impulsive Behavior: Dangerous driving, promiscuous sex, gambling—anything that creates intense sensation or adrenaline.

Workaholism: Staying busy every second so there's no space to feel.

Suicidal Thoughts: The ultimate escape when other Firefighters can't stop the pain.

All of these behaviors share something in common: they're immediate, impulsive, and focused on stopping pain right now, regardless of tomorrow's consequences.

The Difference Between Managers and Firefighters

This is important to understand: Managers try to prevent pain before it happens. Firefighters react after it's already happening.

Managers are like the security team that checks everyone at the door, trying to keep problems out of the building in the first place.

Firefighters are like the emergency team that rushes in when something already got past security and the building is on fire.

Managers are proactive and controlling. Firefighters are reactive and impulsive.

Managers say: "If we do everything right, nothing bad will happen." Firefighters say: "Something bad is happening RIGHT NOW. Do whatever it takes to make it stop."

Let me show you this difference:

Chloe's Two Protectors

Chloe has both strong Managers and strong Firefighters.

Her **Manager** makes her check her bank account multiple times a day, budget carefully, and feel anxious about spending any money. This Manager is trying to prevent financial disaster.

Her **Firefighter** makes her go on shopping binges when she's upset, buying clothes and home decor she doesn't need and can't afford. This Firefighter is trying to stop emotional pain by creating a temporary high.

See the problem? The Manager and Firefighter are working against each other. The Manager tries to control spending. But when an Exile gets triggered and Chloe feels the pain of unworthiness or emptiness, the Firefighter takes over and blows the budget.

Then the Manager comes back and criticizes her: *You're so irresponsible. You'll never get your life together.* This criticism triggers more pain, which activates the Firefighter again, which leads to more shopping.

It's a cycle that keeps Chloe stuck.

Common Firefighter Behaviors

Let's look at some specific Firefighters and the people who have them:

Isaac's Alcohol Firefighter

Isaac is 29 and works in finance. He's successful, responsible, has his life together—at least on the surface. But Thursday through Saturday nights, Isaac drinks heavily. Not just a couple beers—he drinks until he blacks out.

Isaac's coworkers think he's just a party guy. But here's what's actually happening:

Isaac has Exiles that carry deep loneliness and a belief that he's fundamentally unlikable. During the work week, his Managers keep him busy and distracted. But by Thursday evening, the week's stress has weakened his Managers, and the lonely Exiles start pushing through. The feelings are unbearable—a pit in his stomach, a sense that he's completely alone even though he's surrounded by people.

That's when his Firefighter shows up with alcohol. Three drinks in, the pain disappears. The loneliness fades. Isaac feels confident, social, connected. The Firefighter has done its job—the fire is out.

But Monday morning, Isaac wakes up to consequences: hangovers, embarrassing texts he sent, money wasted, a growing sense that he might have a problem. His Managers are furious with the Firefighter. His Inner Critic attacks: *You're pathetic. You can't even control your drinking. What's wrong with you?*

This criticism triggers the Exiles again—*See, you are pathetic and unlikable*—which means by Thursday, the Firefighter will need to show up again.

Isaac's stuck in a loop. The Firefighter is trying to help, but the method creates more problems, which trigger more pain, which require more firefighting.

Natasha's Rage Firefighter

Natasha is 33, married with two kids. She loves her family, but she has a problem: she explodes with rage over small things.

Her daughter spills juice on the carpet, and Natasha screams. Her husband forgets to take out the trash, and she unleashes fury that feels way bigger than the situation warrants. Later, she feels terrible—guilty, ashamed, worried that she's damaging her kids.

What's happening?

Natasha has Exiles that carry helplessness and fear from growing up with a chaotic, alcoholic father. She never knew what would set him off, never felt safe, never had control. Those feelings got buried— exiled—because they were too much for child Natasha to handle.

Now, as an adult, when something happens that makes her feel even slightly out of control—a mess, a forgotten task, kids not listening— those Exile feelings start bubbling up. Her Firefighter rushes in with rage because anger feels powerful. It's the opposite of helpless. When Natasha is raging, she feels in control, even though she's actually out of control.

The rage pushes away the vulnerable feelings of fear and helplessness. The fire is out—temporarily.

But the cost is huge. Her kids are learning to walk on eggshells around her. Her husband is withdrawing. Natasha hates who she becomes when she rages, which triggers shame, which triggers the Exiles more, which means more rage.

The Firefighter is trying to protect her from the terrifying feeling of helplessness, but the method is damaging her relationships and making her feel worse about herself.

Amir's Work Firefighter

Amir is a 36-year-old lawyer who works 70-80 hours a week. He's in the office by 7am, doesn't leave until 8pm, and works most weekends. His friends have stopped inviting him to things because he always cancels. He barely sees his girlfriend. He's exhausted all the time.

People think Amir is just ambitious. But Amir knows something else is going on. He can't stop working. Even when he tries to take time off, he feels intensely anxious and ends up checking email or doing work anyway.

What's happening?

Amir has Exiles that carry a deep sense of worthlessness. These parts developed when Amir was a kid and his parents barely noticed him. They weren't abusive—just checked out, focused on their own problems. Amir learned that he was essentially invisible, which created a belief: *I don't matter. I'm not important.*

As an adult, work became Amir's Firefighter strategy. When he's working, he feels important. He feels needed. Partners email him with urgent questions. Clients depend on him. He matters.

If Amir stops working, the Exile feelings come up: *You don't matter. Nobody actually cares about you. You're not important.* These feelings are unbearable. So the Work Firefighter keeps Amir busy every moment, using productivity to cover the pain of feeling worthless.

The problem? Amir's burning out. His health is suffering. His relationship is falling apart. And despite all his work, that empty feeling is still there underneath, waiting for any moment of stillness.

Brooklyn's Phone Firefighter

Brooklyn is 24. She knows she's on her phone too much—scrolling Instagram, TikTok, Twitter, refreshing email, checking messages.

She picks up her phone without thinking. She scrolls before bed, first thing in the morning, during meals, while watching TV.

Brooklyn has tried to cut back, but she can't. When she puts her phone down for more than a few minutes, she feels uncomfortable, restless, almost panicky. So she picks it back up.

What's the phone doing for Brooklyn?

Brooklyn has Exiles that carry anxiety and a sense that she's missing out, that everyone else's life is better, that she's falling behind. These parts developed during high school when Brooklyn felt like an outsider, watching other girls have the friendships and experiences she wanted.

The phone is a Firefighter that keeps Brooklyn distracted from these painful feelings. When she's scrolling, she's not feeling her own anxiety—she's absorbed in other people's content. The constant stimulation keeps her from sitting with her own thoughts and feelings.

But the scrolling actually makes the problem worse. Seeing everyone's highlight reels triggers the Exiles more: *Everyone else is doing better than you. You're alone. You're behind.* Which means Brooklyn needs to scroll more to numb those feelings.

It's a cycle that keeps her stuck, and she doesn't even realize her phone use is a Firefighter protecting her from painful Exiles.

Why Firefighters Feel Out of Control

Here's what people often say about their Firefighter behaviors:

"I know I shouldn't do it, but I can't stop." "I tell myself I won't do it again, but then I do." "It's like someone else takes over." "I feel powerless against it."

51

This makes sense. Firefighters are emergency responders. They're not interested in your rational thoughts or your long-term goals. They're operating in survival mode, focused only on stopping the pain right now.

Think about what happens when an actual fire alarm goes off in a building. People don't walk calmly toward the exits discussing the best route. They react immediately, sometimes trampling each other in the rush to get out. That's emergency response mode—fast, instinctive, not concerned with niceties.

Your Firefighter parts work the same way. When they perceive an emergency (Exile pain breaking through), they react immediately with whatever works to stop it, regardless of whether it's the best choice.

Firefighters Aren't Trying to Ruin Your Life

Here's what you need to understand: Firefighters, like all parts, have a positive intention. They're trying to protect you from overwhelming pain.

Yes, their methods cause problems. Yes, you'd be better off without binge drinking or rage or compulsive spending. But the Firefighter isn't trying to mess up your life. It's trying to save you from pain it believes will destroy you.

This is so important to understand, because most people's relationship with their Firefighters is all about shame and fighting:

I'm so weak for doing this. I need to just stop. What's wrong with me? I hate this part of myself.

But that approach doesn't work. When you shame and fight the Firefighter, it just digs in harder. It thinks: *You need me even more now because you're in pain about the thing I did to stop your pain.*

The IFS approach is different. Instead of fighting the Firefighter, you get curious about it:

What pain are you trying to protect me from? When did you learn this strategy? What are you afraid will happen if you don't do this behavior?

Let me show you what this looks like:

Luis and His Firefighter

Luis is 41 and has been struggling with emotional eating for years. When he's stressed or upset, he eats—not because he's hungry, but because food temporarily soothes him. He's gained weight, his doctor is concerned about his health, and Luis feels ashamed every time he binges.

Luis has tried willpower, diets, meal plans—nothing works long-term. The Firefighter always wins.

Then Luis learns about IFS. Instead of fighting the eating Firefighter, he tries talking to it:

I know you're trying to help. What pain are you protecting me from?

Luis gets an image of himself at 12 years old, sitting alone at lunch in middle school. He remembers the intense loneliness, the feeling that nobody wanted him around.

The Firefighter shows him: *When you eat, you're not alone. Food is comfort. Food doesn't reject you. I give you something reliable when you feel that old loneliness.*

Luis feels compassion for the Firefighter. It's been working for almost 30 years to protect him from that childhood loneliness. It's not trying to make him unhealthy—it's trying to give him comfort.

Thank you for trying to help, Luis says to the Firefighter. *I get it now. You've been doing this since I was 12, trying to help me not feel so alone.*

That moment of understanding shifts something. Luis isn't cured overnight—that's not how this works. But now when he feels the urge to eat emotionally, he can pause and think: *The Firefighter is showing up because there's a lonely part underneath. What does that part actually need?*

Sometimes he still eats. But sometimes he's able to give that lonely part what it really needs—connection, comfort, acknowledgment—instead of food.

The Relationship Between Managers, Firefighters, and Exiles

Now that you understand all three types of parts, let's look at how they interact:

The Cycle:

1. Something happens that triggers an Exile (a reminder of old pain).
2. Managers try to prevent the Exile feelings from coming up (through controlling, planning, criticizing, etc.).
3. If the Managers can't keep the Exile contained, the feelings start breaking through.
4. Firefighters rush in with impulsive behaviors to shut down the pain immediately.
5. The Firefighter behavior creates consequences (hangovers, debt, broken relationships, shame).
6. Managers criticize you for the Firefighter behavior, which triggers Exiles more.
7. Repeat.

Let me show you this cycle with a complete example:

Grace's Week

Monday: Grace wakes up anxious. Her Planner Manager immediately kicks in, making lists and organizing her week. This helps her feel in control. The anxiety (an Exile trying to come up) gets pushed back down.

Tuesday: Grace's boss criticizes her work in a meeting. An Exile that carries shame and inadequacy gets triggered. Grace's Inner Critic Manager jumps in immediately: *He's right. You're not good enough. You need to work harder.* Grace stays late at the office, trying to prove herself. The Manager is working overtime to prevent the shame from being felt fully.

Wednesday: Grace is exhausted from working late. She's running on coffee and stress. Her Managers are getting tired. That evening, the shame Exile breaks through—she feels worthless, like a failure, like everyone sees how inadequate she is. The feeling is unbearable.

Wednesday night: Grace's Firefighter activates. She goes to Target "just to pick up a few things" and spends $300 on stuff she doesn't need. While she's shopping, the shame disappears. She feels good, excited about her purchases. The Firefighter has successfully distracted her from the pain.

Thursday morning: Grace wakes up and sees her credit card statement. Her Manager immediately attacks: *You're so irresponsible. You can't even control your spending. How are you going to pay rent?* This criticism triggers the inadequacy Exile even more: *See, you really are a failure.*

Thursday evening: The shame is back, even worse now. Grace's Firefighter shows up again—this time with wine. She drinks half a bottle alone in her apartment, scrolling social media. The pain fades.

Friday: Grace wakes up with a headache and regret. The Manager is furious. The cycle continues.

See how it works? The parts are all trying to help, but they're actually keeping Grace stuck in a loop. The Managers try to control everything to prevent pain. When they fail, Firefighters use impulsive behaviors to numb the pain. The Firefighter behaviors create more problems, which the Managers criticize, which triggers more Exile pain, which requires more Firefighting.

Grace isn't weak. She doesn't lack willpower. She's stuck in a cycle where her parts are fighting each other instead of working together.

Breaking the Cycle

The good news: this cycle can be broken. But not by fighting your Firefighters or trying harder to control them.

The cycle breaks when:

1. You get to know your Firefighters with curiosity instead of shame
2. You understand what pain they're protecting you from
3. You help the protective parts (both Managers and Firefighters) trust that your Self can handle the Exile pain
4. You heal the Exiles so they're not carrying so much pain anymore

We'll talk about how to do this in the next chapters. For now, just start noticing your own Firefighters.

Recognizing Your Firefighters

What do you do when you're in pain and want the pain to stop immediately?

Do you drink or use substances? Do you rage or pick fights? Do you binge eat or restrict food? Do you shop or spend money impulsively? Do you scroll social media for hours? Do you work obsessively? Do you have sex impulsively? Do you harm yourself?

Do you drive recklessly or take other risks? Do you shut down completely and go numb?

These aren't character flaws. They're Firefighter strategies— imperfect attempts to protect you from pain.

The first step isn't stopping these behaviors. The first step is recognizing them for what they are: parts of you trying to help in the only way they know how.

In the next chapter, we'll learn a step-by-step process for working with all your parts—Managers, Firefighters, and Exiles. We'll learn the 6 F's, the core protocol that makes IFS work.

Chapter 6: The 6 F's

Your Step-by-Step Guide to Working with Parts

By now, you understand the basics: you have different parts, including Managers who try to prevent pain, Firefighters who react to pain, and Exiles who carry old wounds. You know these parts are all trying to help, even when their methods create problems.

But how do you actually work with parts? How do you talk to them? How do you help them change?

That's what this chapter is about. I'm going to teach you the 6 F's— the step-by-step process that IFS therapists use to work with parts. Think of it as a roadmap for having conversations with your internal family.

Before we start, remember: this is a skill that takes practice. You're not going to be perfect at it right away. That's completely normal. Be patient with yourself as you learn.

The 6 F's: An Overview

The 6 F's are:

1. **Find** the part
2. **Focus** on it
3. **Flesh** it out
4. **Feel** toward it
5. **beFriend** it
6. **Fear** - learn about its fears

Some IFS practitioners add a 7th F: **Find out from the part** what it needs. But we'll stick with the main six for now.

These steps help you separate from a part (unblend), get to know it, and build a relationship with it from your Self. Let's go through each step with detailed examples.

Step 1: Find the Part

The first step is identifying which part you want to work with. This sounds simple, but it's important to be specific.

Instead of just feeling "anxious" or "stressed" or "bad," you want to find the specific part that's bringing that feeling or behavior.

How to Find a Part:

Notice what you're feeling or experiencing right now. Then ask yourself: *What part of me is feeling this?* or *What part of me is doing this?*

You might get a sense of the part immediately. Or you might need to look around inside for it.

Example: Finding Dominic's Anxious Part

Dominic wakes up on Sunday morning feeling a low-level anxiety. It's his day off, but he can't relax. He decides to try working with this feeling using IFS.

He asks: *What part of me is anxious right now?*

He waits and notices. The anxiety seems strongest in his chest—a tight, fluttery feeling. He focuses his attention there and gets a sense of the part: it feels young, maybe 10 or 11 years old, and it's worried about all the things that could go wrong in the week ahead.

Dominic has found the part. It's a young, anxious Manager that worries about the future.

Tips for Finding:

- Notice where you feel something in your body
- Ask which part is most prominent right now
- If multiple parts are present, ask which one wants to talk first
- Sometimes parts announce themselves clearly; sometimes you have to search a bit

Step 2: Focus on the Part

Once you've found the part, you focus your attention on it. This means giving it your full awareness, like turning a spotlight onto that part.

You want to notice as much as you can about the part:

- Where is it in or around your body?
- How intense is it?
- What does it feel like?

How to Focus:

Ask: *Where is this part? How close or far away does it feel? How strong is it?*

Really pay attention to the part, like you're studying it with genuine interest.

Example: Focusing on Dominic's Part

Dominic focuses his attention on the anxious part in his chest. He notices:

- It's located in the center of his chest
- It feels tight and fluttery
- It's pretty strong—maybe a 7 out of 10 in intensity
- It has a forward-leaning quality, like it's trying to rush toward the future

By focusing, Dominic is getting to know the felt sense of this part.

60

Tips for Focusing:

- Take your time—don't rush this step
- Notice physical sensations
- Notice qualities (tight, heavy, hot, cold, moving, still)
- If you get distracted, gently bring your attention back to the part

Step 3: Flesh Out the Part

This is where you get more detail about what the part looks like, how old it is, and what it wants you to know. You're fleshing out the part—giving it more dimension and detail.

How to Flesh Out:

Ask the part questions like:

- *How old are you?*
- *Do you have an image or appearance?*
- *What do you want me to know about you?*
- *How long have you been doing this?*

Example: Fleshing Out Dominic's Part

Dominic asks the anxious part: *How old are you?*

He gets an immediate sense: 11 years old.

Do you have an image?

Dominic sees himself at 11, wearing his middle school uniform, looking worried and small.

What do you want me to know?

The part shows him a memory: Dominic is 11, and he forgot to do a big homework assignment. He got called out by the teacher in front of the whole class. He felt humiliated and terrified. The part says: *I'm trying to make sure that never happens again. I worry about everything so you won't be caught unprepared.*

By fleshing out the part, Dominic understands where it came from and what it's trying to do.

Tips for Fleshing Out:

- Accept whatever comes—don't force specific answers
- Parts might show you memories or just give you a sense of things
- Some people get clear visual images; others get feelings or just knowing
- All ways of experiencing parts are valid

Step 4: Feel Toward the Part

This is the most important step in the whole process. This is where you check to see if your Self is present.

You ask yourself: *How do I feel toward this part?*

If you're in Self, you'll feel some version of the C-qualities we talked about in Chapter 2: curiosity, compassion, calm, clarity, etc.

If you're not in Self—if another part is blended—you'll feel something else: annoyance, fear, judgment, wanting it to go away, frustration, etc.

How to Feel Toward:

Ask yourself: *How do I feel toward this part?*

Notice what comes up. Be honest.

If you feel compassion, curiosity, or care—great! You're in Self. Continue to the next step.

If you feel judgment, annoyance, fear, or wanting it to go away—
that's another part. You need to work with that part first.

Example: Feeling Toward Dominic's Part

Dominic asks himself: *How do I feel toward this anxious 11-year-old part?*

He notices that he feels compassion. He feels sad that this young
part has been working so hard for 20 years, trying to prevent
humiliation. He feels curious about what the part needs.

This tells Dominic he's in Self. He can continue.

Example: When You're Not in Self—Tanya's Experience

Tanya is working with a part that makes her binge eat. She finds the
part, focuses on it, and fleshes it out—it's a Firefighter that uses food
to numb feelings.

Then she asks: *How do I feel toward this part?*

Immediately, she feels disgust and anger. *I hate this part. It's making
me fat. It's ruining my health.*

That's not Self. That's another part—probably an Inner Critic or a
Perfectionist that hates the Firefighter.

Tanya needs to ask this critical part: *Would you be willing to step
back a little so I can talk to the eating part?*

The critical part says: *No way. That part needs to be stopped, not
befriended.*

Tanya then needs to work with the critical part first, asking what it's
afraid of, what it's trying to protect her from. Only after the critical
part relaxes can Tanya access her Self and work with the eating
Firefighter from a place of curiosity instead of judgment.

Tips for Feeling Toward:

- Be completely honest about what you feel
- If it's not compassion or curiosity, you're blended with another part
- Ask the interfering part to step back
- Sometimes you need to work with the interfering part first
- This step can't be faked—parts know if you're really in Self or not

Step 5: beFriend the Part

Once you're in Self and feeling curious or compassionate toward the part, you befriend it. You let it know you see it, you hear it, you appreciate what it's been trying to do.

This is where you build a relationship with the part. You're essentially saying: *I get it. I understand why you're doing this. Thank you for trying to help me.*

How to beFriend:

Say to the part (internally):

- *Thank you for showing yourself to me*
- *I appreciate how hard you've been working*
- *I understand you're trying to help*
- *I'm here to get to know you, not to get rid of you*

Listen to how the part responds.

Example: beFriending Dominic's Part

Dominic says to the anxious part: *Thank you for trying to protect me all these years. I get it now—you've been working since I was 11 to make sure I never feel that humiliation again. That's a long time to carry that responsibility.*

The part seems to soften a bit. Dominic feels it relax slightly in his chest.

I'm not trying to make you go away. I just want to understand you better and see if there's a way I can help.

The part responds (not in words exactly, but Dominic gets the sense): *Really? You're not going to tell me to stop worrying?*

No, Dominic says. *I want to understand why you worry and what you're afraid of.*

The part relaxes more. It feels heard, maybe for the first time.

Tips for beFriending:

- Be genuine—parts can sense insincerity
- Express appreciation for what the part has been trying to do
- Don't promise you'll get rid of the part or make it stop
- Listen to how the part responds
- Building trust takes time

Step 6: Learn About the Part's Fears

Now that you've befriended the part, you ask about its fears. What is it trying to prevent? What's it afraid will happen if it stops doing its job?

This is where you learn what the part is protecting you from. Usually, it's protecting you from Exiles—from feeling old pain.

How to Ask About Fears:

Ask the part:

- *What are you afraid would happen if you didn't do this?*
- *What are you protecting me from?*

- *What would happen if you stopped worrying/controlling/criticizing/etc.?*

Example: Learning Dominic's Part's Fears

Dominic asks the anxious part: *What are you afraid would happen if you stopped worrying about everything?*

The part immediately shows him: *You'd forget something important. You'd be unprepared. You'd get humiliated again, and this time it would be worse because you're an adult. People would see you're a fraud who can't handle his responsibilities.*

So you're trying to protect me from humiliation and from people seeing me as incompetent?

Yes. If I keep you worried and prepared, you'll always be ready. You'll never be caught off guard.

Dominic understands now. The part isn't just randomly anxious. It has a specific job: prevent the humiliation that happened when Dominic was 11.

Is there a younger part—maybe the 11-year-old who got humiliated—that you're protecting?

Yes. That part is still there, still holding that shame. I keep him locked away by making sure nothing like that ever happens again.

Now Dominic sees the full picture. The anxious Manager is protecting an Exile that carries shame from that classroom experience 20 years ago.

Tips for Learning About Fears:

- Parts usually have very specific fears
- The fears often connect to past experiences
- Protective parts are usually protecting Exiles

66

- Listen without judgment
- Validate the part's concerns—they make sense given what it experienced

Putting It All Together: A Complete Example

Let me show you the full 6 F's process with a complete example:

Melissa's Inner Critic

Melissa, 38, decides to work with her Inner Critic—the voice that constantly tells her she's not good enough.

Find: Melissa notices the critical voice has been particularly loud today. She asks: *Which part is being critical?* She gets a sense of a sharp, harsh presence.

Focus: She focuses on the critical part. It feels like it's sitting on her right shoulder, looking down at her with disapproval. It feels heavy and constant.

Flesh Out: Melissa asks: *How old are you?* The part seems adult—maybe 30s. *What do you want me to know?* The part says: *I'm trying to make you better. You keep making mistakes and falling short. Someone has to point out what you need to fix.*

Feel Toward: Melissa asks herself: *How do I feel toward this critical part?* Immediately, she feels annoyed. *I hate this voice. I wish it would shut up.*

Melissa realizes she's not in Self—she's blended with a part that hates the Critic. She asks that part: *Would you step back so I can talk to the Critic?*

The part doesn't want to: *That Critic is mean. It makes you feel terrible.*

Melissa says to this protective part: *I know. But maybe if I understand the Critic better, it won't need to be so harsh. Will you give me a chance to talk to it?*

The protective part agrees to step back a little.

Melissa checks again: *How do I feel toward the Critic now?*

This time, she feels curious. She wonders why this part is so harsh. She's in Self now.

beFriend: Melissa says to the Critic: *I know you've been working really hard, pointing out everything I could improve. That must be exhausting.*

The Critic seems surprised to be acknowledged. It softens just slightly.

I'm not trying to fight you or make you go away. I want to understand what you're trying to do for me.

The Critic responds: *Someone has to keep you in line. If I don't push you, you'll never be good enough.*

Fear: Melissa asks: *Good enough for what? What are you afraid would happen if you stopped criticizing me?*

The Critic says: *You'd become lazy. You'd stop trying. You'd never amount to anything. People would see you're actually mediocre, and you'd be alone and worthless.*

So you're trying to protect me from being worthless and alone?

Yes. If I keep you striving, keep you improving, you'll be valuable. People will want you around.

Is there a younger part that feels worthless and alone? A part you're trying to protect?

The Critic shows her an image: Melissa at 8 years old, sitting alone during recess. She'd been rejected by a group of girls she'd tried to befriend.

That little girl felt so worthless when those girls rejected her. I made sure we'd never feel that way again. I'd make you good enough that nobody would reject you.

Melissa feels compassion—both for the 8-year-old Exile carrying that worthlessness, and for the Critic that's been working for 30 years to prevent that feeling from coming back.

Thank you for trying to protect me from that pain. I see what you've been doing all this time.

What Happens Next?

After you've gone through the 6 F's with a part, you've accomplished something big: you've built a relationship with it. The part feels seen and understood, maybe for the first time.

But this doesn't mean the part immediately changes its behavior. Remember, it's been doing this job for years, maybe decades. It won't just stop because you had one conversation with it.

What happens next is continued relationship-building. You keep checking in with the part. You keep listening to it. And eventually, you work with the part to help it see that your Self can handle things now.

For protective parts (Managers and Firefighters), the goal is to help them trust your Self enough that they can relax and take on different roles. But they won't do that until they trust that the Exiles they're protecting will be taken care of.

That's where the next chapter comes in—healing the Exiles through a process called unburdening.

Practicing the 6 F's

The 6 F's are a skill you develop with practice. Don't expect to be perfect at it right away.

Start with smaller, less intense parts. Don't begin with your most traumatic Exile or your most destructive Firefighter. Practice with a part that's present but not overwhelming—maybe a mild anxious part, or a part that has a small habit you'd like to understand better.

As you practice, the process becomes more natural. You'll start to notice parts more easily. You'll develop your ability to unblend and access Self. You'll get better at listening to what parts need.

Some people find it helpful to write out their conversations with parts. Others prefer to do it purely internally. Some people work with a therapist who guides them through the process. There's no one right way.

The key is patience and compassion—both for your parts and for yourself as you learn this new skill.

In the next chapter, we'll talk about the deepest healing work in IFS: unburdening Exiles so they can let go of the pain they've been carrying for years.

Chapter 7: Healing and Unburdening - The Transformation Process

We've talked about protective parts—the Managers who try to prevent pain and the Firefighters who react to pain. We've learned how to work with these parts using the 6 F's. But we haven't yet talked about the deepest work in IFS: healing the Exiles.

This is where real transformation happens. When Exiles heal—when they release the burdens they've been carrying—the whole system changes. The protective parts can finally relax because they're no longer protecting wounded parts. The cycles you've been stuck in for years can finally break.

This chapter is about that healing process, which IFS calls "unburdening."

What Is Unburdening?

Remember, Exiles carry burdens—painful beliefs and feelings they absorbed during difficult experiences. These burdens are like heavy backpacks full of rocks labeled "I'm worthless," "I'm unlovable," "The world isn't safe," "I'm bad."

Unburdening is the process of helping these parts put down the backpack. It's helping them release the painful beliefs and feelings that aren't actually true about them.

Here's the beautiful thing: when Exiles unburden, they don't disappear. Instead, they transform. They discover who they are without the burden. An Exile that was carrying shame might discover playfulness or creativity. An Exile that was carrying terror might discover peace or courage.

The essence of the part—its fundamental nature—is actually positive. The burdens are like layers of mud covering that positive essence. Unburdening is washing off the mud so the part can shine.

Why This Work Requires Careful Preparation

Before I explain how unburdening works, I need to emphasize something important: you don't go straight to healing Exiles. That would be like rushing into a house that protective parts have been guarding for years.

Remember, protective parts locked away the Exiles because the pain felt too overwhelming. If you try to access Exiles without permission from the protectors, those protectors will fight back—and rightly so. They're doing their job.

This is why so many people who try to "deal with their trauma" without proper support end up feeling worse. They try to bulldoze past the protectors to get to the pain, and the protectors activate even more strongly to prevent that.

The IFS approach is different. We work with protectors first. We build relationships with them. We help them understand that the Self can handle healing the Exiles. We get their permission. And only then—when the protective system trusts that it's safe—do we approach the Exiles.

Think of it like this: Imagine a guard dog has been protecting a wounded child for years. You don't just walk past the guard dog and try to help the child. First, you need to befriend the guard dog, show it you're trustworthy, and get its permission to approach. Otherwise, the dog will attack you, and the child stays wounded.

Your protective parts are like that guard dog. They need to trust you before they'll let you near the Exiles.

The Steps to Healing Exiles

Once protective parts give permission, the unburdening process has several steps:

1. **Witnessing:** The Self witnesses what the Exile experienced
2. **Retrieval:** The Self retrieves the Exile from the past and brings it to safety
3. **Unburdening:** The Exile releases its burdens
4. **Invitation:** The Exile takes on positive qualities to replace the burdens
5. **Integration:** The Exile integrates back into the system in a new role

Let's go through each step with detailed examples.

Step 1: Witnessing

The first step in healing an Exile is witnessing. The Self bears witness to what the Exile experienced—the pain, the fear, the loneliness, whatever it went through.

This isn't about reliving trauma in a overwhelming way. It's about the Self being present with the part, seeing what it went through, and offering the compassion and understanding it needed at the time but didn't get.

Example: Oscar's Exile

Oscar is 44. Through IFS work with a therapist, he's developed relationships with his protective parts—an anxious Manager and a work-obsessed Firefighter. These parts have been protecting an Exile that carries deep loneliness.

The protective parts have finally agreed it's safe for Oscar to approach this Exile.

Oscar focuses inside and asks: *Where is the lonely part?*

He gets an image: he's 7 years old, sitting on the floor of his childhood bedroom, alone. His parents are downstairs fighting loudly.

Oscar's Self asks the 7-year-old: *Can you show me what happened? What you needed me to see?*

The young Exile shows him: nights upon nights of sitting in that room alone, listening to his parents fight, feeling terrified and unwanted. Nobody came to check on him. Nobody explained what was happening. Nobody held him or told him it would be okay.

The Self—adult Oscar—witnesses this. He feels compassion for this scared child who shouldn't have been alone with those feelings.

I see what you went through. I see how scared and lonely you were. I'm so sorry that happened to you.

The 7-year-old feels seen, maybe for the first time. Someone finally acknowledges what he experienced.

This is witnessing: the Self being present with the Exile's experience, seeing it fully, and offering compassion.

Step 2: Retrieval

After witnessing what the Exile experienced, the Self retrieves it from the past. This is a symbolic but powerful process where the Self goes back to where the Exile is stuck and brings it to the present.

Remember, Exiles are often frozen in time—still living in the moment of the original wound. Retrieval helps them understand that the bad thing is over. They're not still there. They're here now, and it's safe.

Example: Oscar's Retrieval

Oscar asks the 7-year-old: *Do you know how old I am now?*

The young part looks up at him, confused. He's been so focused on surviving those scary nights that he doesn't realize time has passed.

I'm 44 now. That was 37 years ago. Those nights are over. You're not still there in that room.

The young part looks around, taking this in.

Would you like to come with me? Out of that room, away from that time? You don't have to stay there anymore.

The 7-year-old nods. Oscar (in his imagination, from his Self) picks up the young part and carries him out of that bedroom, out of that house, away from those scary nights.

He brings the young part to a place that feels safe—Oscar imagines a sunny beach, warm and peaceful. They sit together.

You're safe now. Those nights are in the past. I'm here, and I can take care of you.

The young part begins to relax, understanding for the first time that the bad thing is over.

This is retrieval: bringing the Exile out of the past and into the present, helping it understand that the danger has passed.

Step 3: Unburdening

Now comes the central healing work: helping the Exile release its burdens.

The Self asks the Exile: *What are you carrying that isn't yours to carry? What beliefs or feelings did you pick up from that experience that you'd like to let go of?*

The Exile identifies its burdens—often things like "I'm alone," "I'm unwanted," "I'm not safe," "I'm worthless."

Then the Self helps the Exile release these burdens. This is often done symbolically. The Exile might:

- Wash the burdens away in water
- Burn them in fire
- Release them into light
- Bury them in the earth
- Send them up into the sky

Different people visualize this differently, and that's fine. What matters is the intention: the Exile is letting go of what it's been carrying.

Example: Oscar's Unburdening

Oscar asks the 7-year-old: *What did you learn about yourself during those nights alone? What beliefs did you pick up?*

The young part says: *I'm alone. Nobody wants me. I'm not important enough for anyone to care about.*

Would you like to let go of those beliefs? They're not the truth about you—they're what you picked up from a bad situation. You don't have to carry them anymore.

The young part nods. He wants to let them go.

How would you like to release them?

The young part looks at the ocean in front of them. Oscar helps him visualize the burdens—loneliness, unwantedness, unimportance—as heavy stones. Together, they throw the stones into the ocean. They watch them sink down and disappear.

As each stone disappears, the young part feels lighter. His shoulders relax. His face brightens.

How do you feel now? Oscar asks.

Lighter. Free.

This is unburdening: releasing the painful beliefs and feelings that were never true about the part in the first place.

Step 4: Invitation

After the Exile has released its burdens, there's space for something new. The Self invites the Exile to take on positive qualities to replace what was released.

These aren't forced on the Exile. The Self asks: *What qualities would you like to bring in now? What feels right to you?*

Exiles often choose qualities like joy, peace, playfulness, confidence, safety, love, creativity—things that represent who they really are without the burdens.

Example: Oscar's Invitation

Oscar asks the 7-year-old: *Now that you've let go of loneliness and unwantedness, what would you like to bring in? What qualities feel right for you?*

The young part thinks for a moment. *I want to feel connected. And I want to feel playful again—I used to be playful before things got bad.*

Beautiful. Let's invite those in.

Oscar imagines the qualities of connection and playfulness as warm light. The young part opens his arms and lets the light come in, filling the space where the burdens used to be.

The young part's whole energy shifts. He looks like a normal, happy 7-year-old now—not a traumatized one.

This is invitation: bringing in positive qualities that represent the part's true nature.

Step 5: Integration

The final step is integration. The healed Exile comes back into Oscar's system, but in a new role. It's no longer stuck in the past, no longer carrying pain. It can contribute its positive qualities to Oscar's life.

Example: Oscar's Integration

Oscar asks the now-healed young part: *What role would you like to have in my life now?*

The part says: *I want to help you remember to play. And I want to help you connect with people—really connect, not just go through the motions.*

I'd love that. Will you come with me? Be part of my life in that way?

The young part agrees. Oscar imagines welcoming him fully into his heart.

This is integration: the healed Exile taking on a positive, healthy role in your system.

What Changes After Unburdening

When an Exile unburdens, the effects ripple through the whole system:

Protective parts can relax. They've been working so hard to protect the wounded Exile. Now that the Exile is healed, they don't need to work so hard anymore.

Firefighter behaviors decrease. Firefighters react when Exiles break through. If the Exiles aren't in pain anymore, there's less need for emergency firefighting.

Manager parts become less extreme. Managers don't need to control everything or prevent everything if there's no overwhelming pain to prevent.

You feel more like yourself. With less internal conflict and less energy going to protect wounds, you have more access to your Self.

Let me show you what this looks like:

Oscar After Unburdening

Before healing his lonely Exile, Oscar was stuck in patterns. His anxious Manager kept him constantly worried about relationships—checking his phone obsessively, analyzing every interaction, panicking if someone didn't respond quickly. His work Firefighter kept him busy 80 hours a week so he wouldn't feel the loneliness.

After unburdening the 7-year-old Exile, things shifted.

His anxious Manager relaxed. It didn't disappear—Oscar still notices it sometimes—but it's not as intense or constant. Oscar can now go several hours without checking his phone and not feel panic.

His work Firefighter also dialed back. Oscar still works hard, but he doesn't need to work 80 hours a week to avoid feelings anymore. He can actually leave work at the office sometimes.

Most importantly, Oscar feels more capable of real connection. That 7-year-old part that now carries connection and playfulness helps Oscar be more authentic with people. He's not constantly bracing for rejection because the part that carried that fear has healed.

Oscar isn't "cured"—that's not how this works. He still has hard days. His parts still show up. But the system is less extreme, less desperate, more balanced.

Working With Multiple Exiles

Most people have more than one Exile. You might have a part that carries shame from one experience, another that carries fear from a different experience, another that carries grief, and so on.

You don't have to unburden all your Exiles at once. In fact, you can't—it wouldn't be safe or productive.

You work with them one at a time, usually starting with the ones that are most accessible and least overwhelming. As each Exile heals, the system becomes more stable, making it safer to work with other Exiles.

Think of it like cleaning a hoarder's house. You don't try to clear everything in one day. You start with one room, make it functional, then move to the next.

When to Seek Professional Help

I want to be direct about something: unburdening Exiles is deep work. While some people can do elements of it on their own, especially with less intense wounds, many people benefit from having a trained IFS therapist guide the process.

Here's when you should definitely work with a professional:

- If you have a history of significant trauma (abuse, violence, severe neglect)
- If you have suicidal Firefighters or self-harm behaviors
- If you dissociate or have difficulty staying present
- If you feel overwhelmed when you try to work with Exiles
- If your protective parts strongly resist the work
- If you're not able to access Self reliably

There's no shame in needing support. This is hard work. A good IFS therapist knows how to work with your protective parts, create safety, and guide the unburdening process in a way that doesn't retraumatize you.

The Beauty of Unburdening

Here's what makes unburdening so powerful: you're not trying to fix parts or make them different. You're helping them discover who they actually are without the weight of old pain.

That Exile carrying shame? Underneath the shame, it might be joyful and creative.

That Exile carrying terror? Underneath the terror, it might be brave and curious.

That Exile carrying worthlessness? Underneath that belief, it might be confident and full of value.

The burdens were never the truth. They were just heavy layers of pain covering up the part's true nature.

When those layers come off, the part can finally be itself. And when your parts can be themselves—when they're not stuck in extreme roles trying to prevent or react to pain—you can be yourself too.

That's the promise of IFS: not that you'll become someone new, but that you'll become more fully who you already are underneath all the protection and pain.

In the final chapter, we'll talk about how to take everything you've learned and apply it to daily life—in relationships, at work, with anxiety and depression, and in building a sustainable IFS practice.

Chapter 8: Living with IFS –

Practical Applications for Everyday Life

You've learned the theory. You understand parts. You know about the Self, Managers, Firefighters, and Exiles. You've learned the 6 F's for working with parts and the unburdening process for healing them.

Now comes the important question: how do you actually live with this knowledge? How do you use IFS in your daily life—not just in therapy sessions or when you're sitting quietly working with your parts, but in the messy reality of relationships, work stress, parenting, and all the other challenges life throws at you?

This chapter is about practical application. We're going to look at how to use IFS in real-world situations, how to build a daily practice, and how to keep growing with this approach.

Using IFS in Relationships

Relationships are where our parts show up most intensely. Your partner, family members, close friends—these people trigger parts in you, and you trigger parts in them. Understanding this changes everything.

The Dance of Parts

When you're in conflict with someone, it's usually not your Self talking to their Self. It's your parts talking to their parts.

Maybe your anxious Manager is talking to their defensive Firefighter. Maybe your critical Manager is talking to their shame-filled Exile. Parts talking to parts creates escalation and misunderstanding. Self talking to Self creates connection and resolution.

Example: Jenna and Marcus

Jenna and Marcus have been together for five years. They love each other, but they keep having the same fight:

Marcus comes home from work and wants alone time to decompress. Jenna feels hurt and rejected when he retreats to his computer without talking to her first.

Here's what's really happening:

Marcus's side: When Marcus gets home, he's overwhelmed from the day. An Exile that carries feelings of being intruded upon (from growing up with hovering parents) gets activated. His Firefighter responds by withdrawing—he needs space immediately. When Jenna approaches him for connection, his Firefighter sees her as a threat to his desperately needed space. He pulls away harder.

Jenna's side: When Marcus pulls away, Jenna's Exile that carries abandonment (her dad was emotionally distant) gets triggered. This part feels: *He doesn't want me. I'm not important to him.* Her anxious Manager activates, trying to get reassurance from Marcus. The more he pulls away, the more anxious she gets, and the more she pursues him.

See the dance? Marcus's Firefighter triggers Jenna's Exile, which activates Jenna's Manager, which triggers Marcus's Exile more, which activates his Firefighter more. They're stuck in a cycle where parts are reacting to parts.

The IFS Solution:

Jenna and Marcus learn about their parts. They start recognizing when they're in the cycle.

Now, when Marcus comes home, he can notice: *My Firefighter wants to withdraw. But let me check—is Jenna actually intruding, or am I reacting from an old place?*

From his Self, Marcus might say: "Hey, I need 20 minutes to decompress. A part of me is feeling overwhelmed from work. But I want to connect with you after that. Can we have dinner together in half an hour?"

When Marcus says this, Jenna can notice: *My abandonment part is getting triggered. But Marcus isn't actually abandoning me. He's just needing space, and he's already planning to connect soon.*

From her Self, Jenna might say: "Okay, take your time. That part of me that worries you don't want me around is feeling nervous, but I know that's not true. I'll start dinner, and we can catch up when you're ready."

See the difference? They're both acknowledging their parts but speaking from Self. They're not letting the parts run the whole interaction.

Tips for Using IFS in Relationships:

- Notice when you're getting triggered and pause before reacting
- Ask yourself: *Which part of me is activated right now?*
- Share with your partner from Self: "A part of me is feeling [triggered/scared/angry], but I know that's about old stuff. Can we talk about what's actually happening?"
- Get curious about what parts your partner's behavior might be triggering in you
- Remember that your partner's reactions are probably coming from their parts too, not from who they really are

IFS for Anxiety

Anxiety is almost always a Manager part that's trying to protect you by scanning for threats and preparing for worst-case scenarios.

Example: Riley's Presentation Anxiety

Riley has to give a presentation at work. For three days beforehand, she's consumed with anxiety. She can't sleep well. She keeps imagining everything that could go wrong. She's practiced her presentation 20 times but still doesn't feel ready.

Without IFS thinking: Riley would either try to power through the anxiety or beat herself up for being anxious. *Why am I like this? Other people don't get this nervous. Just get over it.*

With IFS thinking: Riley recognizes this is a part. She takes time to talk to it:

What part of me is so anxious about this presentation?

She gets an image of herself at 16, giving a presentation in high school. She blanked completely, stood there frozen while classmates stared. It was humiliating.

So you're the part that's still trying to prevent that humiliation from happening again?

Yes. If we prepare enough, if we think through every possible problem, maybe we can avoid that feeling of being exposed and incompetent.

I understand. That was a terrible experience. Thank you for trying to protect me from feeling that way again. But I'm not 16 anymore. I'm actually good at my job. I've given successful presentations before. I don't need to imagine every worst-case scenario to be prepared.

But what if you forget what you're going to say?

If that happens, I'll handle it. I'll take a breath, look at my notes, and keep going. Adults don't usually get as cruel about mistakes as teenagers do. And I have the skills to recover even if I stumble.

The anxious part doesn't completely disappear—that's not realistic. But it dials down from a 9 to about a 5. Riley can function. She can sleep a bit better. She's not consumed by the anxiety because she's in relationship with it, not taken over by it.

Tips for Using IFS with Anxiety:

- Recognize anxiety as a protective part, not the truth about your situation
- Thank the part for trying to protect you
- Ask what it's afraid of and where it learned to be this worried
- From your Self, reassure the part that you can handle things
- Don't fight the anxiety; work with it

IFS for Depression

Depression often involves Exiles that are blending with you—parts carrying old pain that have broken through and taken over.

It can also involve Firefighter parts that are numbing you out, making you shut down to avoid feeling pain.

Example: Andre's Depression

Andre has been feeling depressed for months. He has no energy. He doesn't want to do things he used to enjoy. He feels empty and hopeless. He's been forcing himself through his days but feeling increasingly numb.

Without IFS thinking: Andre might see depression as something wrong with his brain chemistry (which can be part of it) or as a personal failure. *I should be able to snap out of this. I'm weak.*

With IFS thinking: Andre gets curious about what's happening inside.

What parts are involved in this depression?

He discovers several things:

There's an Exile that carries deep sadness and loneliness from his childhood. This part has been trying to get his attention for years, but Andre's Managers kept pushing it away because the feelings were too painful.

Recently, life stress weakened Andre's Managers enough that the Exile started breaking through. The sadness began flooding his system.

A Firefighter responded by shutting Andre down completely—making him numb so he wouldn't have to feel the Exile's pain. This Firefighter's strategy is: *If we don't feel anything, we won't feel the sad thing.*

The depression is what happens when this Firefighter takes over: numbness, lack of interest, disconnection from life.

Andre's Path:

With help from a therapist, Andre starts working with his protective parts. He helps his Managers and Firefighters understand that his Self can handle the sad Exile—he doesn't need to be protected from it with numbness.

Slowly, carefully, Andre approaches the sad Exile. He witnesses the loneliness this part experienced. He unburdens it. The part releases the old pain.

As the Exile heals, Andre's depression lifts. The Firefighter doesn't need to numb him out anymore because there's less pain to numb. Andre feels things again—both difficult feelings and good ones.

Important Note: Depression can have biological components. Some people need medication in addition to therapy. IFS doesn't replace medical treatment—it works alongside it. If you're experiencing depression, talk to both a therapist and a doctor.

Tips for Using IFS with Depression:

- Recognize that depression often involves exiled parts that need attention
- Notice if a Firefighter is creating numbness
- Work with a professional if depression is severe or persistent
- Be gentle—healing takes time
- Consider whether medication might be helpful alongside IFS work

IFS in the Workplace

Your parts don't stay home when you go to work. They show up in meetings, in interactions with colleagues, in how you approach your tasks.

Common Workplace Parts:

The Perfectionist: Makes you redo work endlessly, afraid anything less than perfect will be criticized

The People-Pleaser: Makes you say yes to everything, unable to set boundaries

The Imposter: Convinced you're a fraud who will be exposed

The Overachiever: Pushes you to work constantly to prove your worth

The Avoider: Procrastinates on difficult tasks because a part is scared of failure

Example: Taylor's Imposter Part

Taylor just got promoted to manager. She's thrilled but also terrified. In meetings, when her boss asks her opinion, a part of her thinks: *Everyone's going to realize I don't know what I'm doing. I'm not qualified for this role. I just got lucky.*

This Imposter part makes Taylor second-guess every decision, over-prepare for every meeting, and stay quiet even when she has valuable input.

Taylor's IFS Approach:

Taylor recognizes this as a part. She takes time to get to know it.

The part is protecting an Exile that carries a belief from childhood: *You're not as smart as everyone thinks. You're fooling people.*

This belief developed because Taylor's older sister was obviously brilliant—straight A's, academic awards, everyone praising her intelligence. Taylor did fine in school, but she wasn't the star her sister was. A part of her absorbed the belief that she was less than, that any success she had was luck rather than capability.

Taylor works with this Exile, helping it see that she has genuine skills and intelligence. She doesn't have to be her sister. Her success isn't luck.

As the Exile heals, the Imposter part relaxes. Taylor starts speaking up more in meetings. She trusts her judgment. She can accept the promotion as something she earned, not something she fooled people into giving her.

Tips for Using IFS at Work:

- Notice which parts show up in work situations
- Take bathroom breaks to check in with activated parts
- Before important meetings, ask your parts to give you space so your Self can lead
- Recognize when colleagues are operating from their parts, not their Self—it's not personal

IFS for Parenting

Parenting activates every part you have. Your kids will trigger your Exiles, activate your Managers, and sometimes bring out your Firefighters.

Understanding this helps you parent from Self instead of from reactive parts.

Example: Diana's Parenting Parts

Diana's 6-year-old son, Ethan, is having a meltdown in the grocery store. He wanted a toy, Diana said no, and now he's screaming and crying on the floor.

Diana's parts activate:

Her **Inner Critic** says: *Everyone's staring at you. They think you're a bad mom who can't control her kid.*

Her **People-Pleaser** says: *Just buy him the toy so he stops. You're disturbing everyone.*

Her **Exile** from childhood remembers being in public with her own mother, who would get angry when Diana misbehaved. The Exile feels shame and fear.

Her **Firefighter** wants to respond with anger: *Stop this right now!*

If Diana reacts from these parts, she'll either give in (which teaches Ethan that tantrums work) or yell at him (which escalates the situation and damages their connection).

Diana from Self:

Diana takes a breath. She notices all these parts activating but doesn't let them take over.

From her Self, she can see: Ethan is 6. He's disappointed and doesn't have great emotional regulation skills yet. This is developmentally normal. Other people's opinions don't actually matter here. Her job is to help Ethan learn to handle disappointment, not to stop his feelings or give in to them.

She kneels down to his level and says calmly: "I know you're really upset that we're not getting that toy. It's hard when you want something and the answer is no. I'm going to stay right here with you while you have these big feelings."

She doesn't cave. She doesn't yell. She stays present, which is what Ethan actually needs.

After a few minutes, Ethan's tantrum winds down. Diana helps him up, they finish shopping, and later that evening she talks with him about feelings and disappointment.

Tips for Using IFS in Parenting:

- Notice when your kids trigger your own Exiles
- Take breaths before responding to challenging behavior
- Ask yourself: *Which part wants to respond here? What would Self do?*
- Recognize that your kids have parts too—their behavior comes from parts, not from who they really are
- Model Self-energy for your kids; they learn emotional regulation from watching you

Building a Daily IFS Practice

IFS isn't just something you do in therapy. It's a way of living—a way of being in relationship with yourself and others.

Here's how to build a sustainable practice:

Morning Check-In (5 minutes):

Before you start your day, take a moment to check in with your parts.

How am I feeling this morning? What parts are present? What do they need from me today?

Maybe your anxious part is already worried about your meeting this afternoon. You can say: *I hear you. We'll prepare for that meeting, but right now, let's focus on breakfast.*

Mindful Pauses:

Throughout the day, pause and notice what's happening inside. Especially when you're triggered or stressed:

What part is activated right now? What does it need?

These don't have to be long—even 30 seconds of awareness helps.

Evening Reflection (10 minutes):

Before bed, reflect on your day.

What parts showed up today? Were there moments when I was in Self? Moments when parts took over? Is there a part that needs attention before I sleep?

This isn't about judging yourself for times parts took over. It's about building awareness and relationship with your internal family.

Deeper Sessions (Weekly):

Set aside 20-30 minutes once a week for deeper work with parts. Use the 6 F's to have conversations with parts that need more attention.

This could be:

- Checking in with a part you've been working with
- Getting to know a new part that's been showing up
- Working on a specific issue or behavior

- Journaling your conversations with parts

Tips for Sustaining Practice:

- Start small—don't try to do everything at once
- Be consistent rather than perfect
- Notice progress without expecting rapid transformation
- Consider working with an IFS therapist for support
- Connect with IFS communities online or in person
- Read books and listen to podcasts about IFS to deepen your understanding

IFS for Life Transitions

Life transitions—changing jobs, moving, relationship changes, health issues, aging—activate parts intensely.

Example: Nina's Job Loss

Nina, 42, gets laid off from a job she's had for 10 years. She's devastated.

Multiple parts activate:

Her **Exile** feels worthless: *See, you weren't valuable enough to keep.*

Her **Anxious Manager** panics about finances: *How will you pay bills? What if you can't find another job?*

Her **Firefighter** wants to numb out with wine and Netflix: *Don't think about it. Just escape.*

Nina's IFS Approach:

Nina recognizes these parts. She makes space for all of them.

To the **Exile**: *I know you feel worthless right now. Layoffs happen for lots of reasons—usually financial, not about individual value. You are valuable, even though you lost this job.*

To the **Anxious Manager**: *I hear your worry about money. That's a real concern. Let's make a plan—look at savings, update my resume, start networking. Having a plan will help you feel less panicked.*

To the **Firefighter**: *I know you want to help me avoid this pain. A little Netflix is okay, but numbing out completely won't help. I need to feel this loss and then move forward.*

Nina doesn't suppress her grief about losing the job. She lets herself feel it, which is what her Self can do. But she doesn't let the Exile's belief that she's worthless take over. She doesn't let the Manager's panic paralyze her. She doesn't let the Firefighter numb her for weeks.

She moves through the transition with all her parts acknowledged but her Self leading.

Recognizing Progress

How do you know if IFS is working? Progress doesn't always look dramatic. Often, it's subtle:

- You notice parts faster
- You can unblend more quickly
- You access Self more easily
- Your parts trust you more
- Patterns that used to trap you for weeks now only trap you for days or hours
- You have more compassion for yourself
- Your relationships improve
- You feel more like yourself

Example: Jordan's Progress

Jordan has been working with IFS for a year. Here's what's changed:

Before: When his girlfriend criticized something he did, Jordan would immediately feel crushed and worthless for days. He'd withdraw and get defensive.

After: When his girlfriend offers feedback now, Jordan still feels a twinge of hurt. But he can pause and think: *That's my shame Exile getting triggered. She's not saying I'm worthless—she's expressing a preference about one specific thing.*

He can say: "A part of me just felt really criticized by that, but I want to hear what you're saying. Can you tell me more about what you need?"

That's progress. Not perfection—he still feels the trigger. But he's not consumed by it. He can stay present instead of disappearing into protective reactions.

Common Challenges

"I can't find my parts." This usually means you're trying too hard. Parts show up naturally when you're relaxed and curious. Try noticing feelings in your body, or pay attention to repetitive thoughts.

"My parts won't talk to me." Parts need to trust you before they open up. Keep showing up. Keep being curious. Trust builds over time.

"I can't access Self." There might be a part blended with you that you haven't noticed. Ask: *What part is blocking access to Self right now?* Work with that part first.

"This isn't working fast enough." Parts have been doing their jobs for years or decades. They won't change overnight. Healing happens at its own pace. Trying to rush it usually makes parts more protective.

"I feel worse since starting IFS." Sometimes awareness of parts makes you more conscious of internal conflict you'd been ignoring. This can feel worse temporarily, but it's actually progress—you're seeing what's been there all along. If it feels overwhelming, work with a therapist.

Next Steps in Your IFS Journey

This book is just the beginning. Here are ways to continue:

Read more:

- "No Bad Parts" by Richard Schwartz
- "Internal Family Systems Therapy" by Richard Schwartz
- "Greater Than the Sum of Our Parts" by Richard Schwartz

Find a therapist: Look for IFS-trained therapists at www.ifs-institute.com

Join communities: Connect with others learning IFS through online forums, local groups, or social media

Take courses: The IFS Institute offers online courses for both professionals and individuals

Practice: Keep working with your parts. The more you practice, the more natural it becomes.

Final Thoughts

IFS offers something beautiful: a way to stop fighting yourself.

Most of us spend so much energy trying to get rid of parts we don't like, trying to control our reactions, trying to be different than we are. IFS says: what if you stopped fighting? What if you got curious about why you're the way you are? What if all those parts you're trying to eliminate are actually trying to help you?

You don't have to be fixed because you're not broken. You're a system of parts that developed strategies to survive and cope with life. Some of those strategies don't work well anymore. Some parts are still responding to old threats that don't exist now. Some parts are carrying pain that needs healing.

But underneath all of that, your Self is there—whole, compassionate, capable. When you can access that Self and let it lead, your parts can relax. They can transform. They can take on new roles that serve you better.

This is the work: getting to know your internal family, helping them trust you, healing the wounded ones, and letting the protective ones know they don't have to work so hard anymore.

It's not easy work. It takes time, patience, and compassion. But it's worth it.

Because on the other side of this work is freedom—freedom from being hijacked by your reactions, freedom from being stuck in old patterns, freedom to be who you actually are underneath all the protection and pain.

Your internal family has been waiting for you to show up as the Self, as the leader they need. They've been doing their best without your leadership, which is why things feel chaotic sometimes.

But now you know how to lead. You know how to listen to parts, understand them, work with them. You know how to access Self and let it guide your internal system.

So start where you are. Notice one part today. Get curious about it. Thank it for trying to help. See what happens.

Your internal family is ready to meet you. All you have to do is show up with curiosity and compassion.

Welcome to your IFS journey.

References

Anderson, F. G., Sweezy, M., & Schwartz, R. C. (2017). *Internal Family Systems skills training manual: Trauma-informed treatment for anxiety, depression, PTSD & substance abuse.* PESI Publishing & Media.

Böckler, A., Herrmann, L., Trautwein, F. M., Holmes, T., & Singer, T. (2017). Know thy selves: Learning to understand oneself increases the ability to understand others. *Journal of Cognitive Enhancement, 1*(2), 197-209.

Comeau, A., Bish, M., & Haliburn, J. (2024). Internal Family Systems therapy for posttraumatic stress disorder: A pilot study of group and individual formats. *Journal of Trauma & Dissociation, 25*(1), 87-104.

Deacon, S. A., & Davis, J. C. (2001). Internal Family Systems therapy with an adolescent and her family struggling with obsessive-compulsive disorder. *Journal of Family Psychotherapy, 12*(3), 55-72.

Green, T. L. (2008). Self leadership in couples: A model for treating couples affected by trauma. *Counselling, Psychotherapy, and Health, 4*(1), 62-81.

Haddock, S. A., Weiler, L. M., Trump, L. J., & Henry, K. L. (2017). The efficacy of Internal Family Systems therapy in the treatment of depression among female college students: A pilot study. *Journal of Marital and Family Therapy, 43*(1), 131-144.

Hodgdon, H. B., Anderson, F. G., Southwell, E., Hrubec, W., & Schwartz, R. C. (2022). Internal Family Systems (IFS) therapy for posttraumatic stress disorder (PTSD) among survivors of multiple childhood trauma: A pilot effectiveness study. *Journal of Aggression, Maltreatment & Trauma, 31*(1), 22-43.

Mones, A. G., & Schwartz, R. C. (2007). The use of the Internal Family Systems model with a sexually abused adolescent. *Journal of Family Psychotherapy, 18*(3), 1-21.

Pais, S. (2009). A systemic approach to the treatment of dissociative identity disorder: A case study using the Internal Family Systems model. *Journal of Trauma & Dissociation, 10*(1), 86-98.

Schwartz, R. C. (1995). *Internal Family Systems therapy*. Guilford Press.

Schwartz, R. C. (2013). Moving from acceptance toward transformation with Internal Family Systems therapy (IFS). *Journal of Clinical Psychology, 69*(8), 805-816.

Schwartz, R. C. (2021). *No bad parts: Healing trauma and restoring wholeness with the Internal Family Systems model*. Sounds True.

Schwartz, R. C., & Sweezy, M. (2020). *Internal Family Systems therapy* (2nd ed.). Guilford Press.

Shadick, N. A., Sowell, N. F., Frits, M. L., Hoffman, S. M., Hartz, S. A., Booth, F. D., Sweezy, M., Rogers, P. R., Dubin, R. L., Atkinson, J. C., Friedman, A. L., Augusto, F., Iannaccone, C. K., Kieval, R. I., Cui, J., Blouin, V., Gravallese, E. M., Schned, E. S., & Weinblatt, M. E. (2013). A randomized controlled trial of an Internal Family Systems-based psychotherapeutic intervention on outcomes in rheumatoid arthritis: A proof-of-concept study. *The Journal of Rheumatology, 40*(11), 1831-1841.

Sweezy, M., & Ziskind, E. L. (Eds.). (2013). *Internal Family Systems therapy: New dimensions*. Routledge.